Affordable
Remodel

Affordable Remodel

HOW TO GET CUSTOM RESULTS ON ANY BUDGET

FERNANDO PAGÉS RUIZ

The Taunton Press

This book, as with all my endeavors, is dedicated to my beautiful wife and best friend, Deborah A. Pagés;

my sons, Fernando and Alejandro; and my parents, Myrtha Elba Ruiz de Pagés and Fernando Pagés Larraya.

ACKNOWLEDGMENTS

LIKE A REMODELING PROJECT, this book came together through the efforts of many skilled craftsmen. In particular, I want to thank Steve Culpepper, who coined the idea for this book; and Robyn Doyon-Aitken, who helped us stay organized, on time, and in good spirits.

I also owe a debt of gratitude to my friends in the remodeling industry, who provided many of the money-saving tips and insights contained here. In particular, I want to mention my friend and colleague Larry Douglas. I thank remodeling luminaries William Asdal of Asdal Builders, New Jersey, Carl Seville, and SawHorse Construction of Atlanta. Architects Jim Zack of Zack de Vito Architecture, Garry L. Martin, and Jerry Berggren of Berggren Architects. For technical help, I called on Jay Crandell of Applied Residential Engineering, Liza Bowles Newport Partners, and the National Association of Homebuilders Research Center.

Perhaps the biggest debt of gratitude is to all of those who opened their homes, including Robert and Sherry Hampton, Judy-Quade Anderson, Paul W. Essman, Heather Callam, Ritch Paprocki, Robert Ormsby, Jr.,Deborah Hall, Lisa and Matt Inness, and my dear mom Myrtha Pagés.

The Taunton Press, Inc., 63 South Main Street, PO Box 5506, Newtown, CT 06470-5506
e-mail: tp@taunton.com

Editor: Roger Yepsen, Steve Culpepper
Jacket/Cover design: Kimberly Adis
Interior design and layout: Kimberly Adis
Illustrator: Robert LaPointe
Photographers: Roger Bruhn and Fernando Pagés Ruiz, unless otherwise noted. Photos by Roger Bruhn: pp. 2 left, 3, 7, 8 top, 10 bottom, 15, 20, 21 bottom right, 22 right, 23 left, 26 top, 27 bottom, 29 bottom, 32 bottom right, 33 bottom right, 36 right, 38 bottom & right, 49, 52 bottom, 54–56, 59, 72, 75, 77 bottom, 87 bottom, 96 sidebar & bottom, 104 top left, 114 bottom, 118, 129 left, 130, 134 bottom, 136 right, 138 left, 155 left, 156 left, 157 top right & bottom right, 161, 162 top left, middle & right, 175, 176 left, 179, 192 top right, 194 bottom right. Photos by Fernando Pagés Ruiz: pp. v top left, 2 right, 5 bottom, 6, 8 bottom left & right, 10 top, 11, 16 bottom, 17, 22 left, 23 right, 25, 26 bottom, 29 top, 31 bottom, 32 top & bottom left, 34, 35, 36 left, 38 top, 40, 41, 42 top & bottom left, 53, 60, 63, 67, 69, 75 bottom, 78–80, 82–85, 86 bottom, 87 top, 89–91, 92 left, 96 top right, 97–101, 104 bottom, 106, 108–109, 110 left, 112 top left & bottom left, 114 top right, 116 top, 120 left, 125 bottom right, 126 bottom right, 127, 131, 135, 136 eft, 137 right, 139, 145 top right, 146 left, 147 left, 148, 152, 155 right, 156 top right & bottom right, 158 bottom left, 170 right, 173, 178 top right, 181 top right & bottom, 187 top left, 189 right, 192 top left, 193 top left, 194 top right, 195, 196 top right & bottom left, 199 right, 202, 203 left & middle, 208 bottom, 209 top, 210, 215.

Library of Congress Cataloging-in-Publication Data
Ruiz, Fernando Pages.
  Affordable remodel : how to get custom results on any budget / Fernando Pagés Ruiz.
    p. cm.
  Includes index.
  ISBN 978-1-56158-846-6
1. Dwellings--Remodeling--Cost control. I. Title.

TH4816.R843 2007
643'.7--dc22

                      2007003174

FOREWORD

OUR NATION HAS MADE TREMENDOUS PROGRESS in boosting the quality of life for American families, with huge increases in new construction and with more people than ever living in safe and decent housing.

Another important trend has been less chronicled, however, and that's the phenomenon of Americans acting upon their own needs through remodeling. We see evidence of those massive efforts in updated homes, in the quality of construction materials, in cost-saving and energy-saving features, and in increased home values. But we can also track the scale of this remodeling explosion in the revenues and profitability of the remodeling industry, from contractors to major retailers.

In *Affordable Remodel*, Fernando Pagés makes it possible for the vast national remodeling phenomenon to reach even deeper into communities and empower people to lovingly invest their ingenuity and elbow grease in their own homes. The book provides a guide for those families who want to personally take on the task of improving and enhancing the value of their homes, whether by planning and overseeing the remodel or by doing the work themselves. Personal creativity and manpower are transformed into practical utility for a family's own purposes, and translate into measurable economic value if the home is sold.

By sharing his experience and insights with a national audience, Fernando Pagés provides a way for individuals to make a better life for their own families and at the same time to make substantial contributions to the improvement of communities and to strengthen the nation as a whole.

—Henry Cisneros, Executive Chairman, CityView, and former
Secretary of Housing and Urban Development

CONTENTS

INTRODUCTION

I HAVE SPENT THE BETTER PART OF my 30-year construction career focused on achieving high-end looks with pocket change. Call me cheap, but I have enjoyed building and also living in luxury homes that don't pull at the purse strings. If you also covet architecture slightly beyond your means, take heart—there are ways to live the good life affordably. The chapters ahead reveal many of the money-saving options available in remodeling today. I discovered some of these techniques and materials while remodeling my own properties and others by interviewing top remodeling contractors around the country. With the power of insider knowledge you too will find ways to achieve the home of your dreams without violating your budget.

1

Strategic Planning

YEARS AGO, YOU COULD REMODEL your house without a lot of planning and soul searching. The decisions were practical, based on making the home larger, easier to live in, and more comfortable. You faced only a few choices in styles and materials, and your house represented a backdrop for cozy living more than a means to prosperity.

Things have changed, however. Over the past 30 years, remodeling has burgeoned into a $200-billion-a-year industry, offering a bewildering excess of upgrades and options. When you consider that homeowners recover only a fraction of improvement costs, on average, when they sell their homes, it becomes obvious just how important harnessing the budget is when you remodel.

Although low interest rates and escalating home equity have lulled consumers into spending more money on remodeling every year, it makes sense to invest only where you can relish the

You can save money when remodeling by getting involved in each stage of the process. That's true whether you do it all yourself, choose subcontractors to take on certain jobs, or hire a pro to run the whole show.

results as well as increase the home's value. If a remodeling project doesn't promise to do either, you should reconsider it. By approaching remodeling with an educated eye focused on savings, you can buck the averages and earn a handsome return on your investment even as you enjoy better living.

The old adage "You get what you pay for" doesn't always hold true in remodeling, where a hyperactive home-improvement industry pushes pricey but often useless upgrades. In the chapters that follow, you will learn how to sort through sales pitches and take charge of your budget while making the best of the choices offered by a competitive marketplace.

FACING REALITY

You probably have already decided to remodel, or you wouldn't be reading this book. Nevertheless, it pays to acknowledge the hazards of what lies ahead: Nothing is more discouraging than realizing you are in over your head when only halfway into

REMODELING VS. RELOCATING

Should you remodel or would it be wiser economically to move? Here are some statistics to consider when making this big decision.

THE RETURN ON VARIOUS HOUSEHOLD IMPROVEMENTS

	JOB COST	RESALE VALUE	COST RECOUPED
Basement remodel	$47,888	$36,475	70.8%
Major kitchen remodel	$42,600	$33,890	79.4%
Added bathroom	$41,587	$33,747	81.1%
Window replacement	$9,273	$7,839	84.5%
Bathroom remodel	$47,888	$8,887	90.1%
Minor kitchen remodel	$47,888	$14,195	92.9%

Source: *REMODELING* magazine, "Cost vs. Value Report," © 2005 by Hanley Wood, LLC.

COST OF SELLING A HOUSE AND MOVING

	NATIONAL AVERAGE	PER $100,000
Real estate commission	6%	$6,000
Closing costs	1.5%	$1,500
Moving expense	3%	$3,000
TOTAL	10.5%	$10,500

Source: *REMODELING* magazine, "Cost vs. Value Report," © 2005 by Hanley Wood, LLC.

APPROACH YOUR REMODELING PROJECT as an opportunity to add value without spending foolishly—to live better and contribute to your nest egg.

TO MOVE OR NOT TO MOVE

The reasons for remodeling almost always start with, "I love the neighborhood, but . . ." And the reasons for moving generally have to do with location.

REASONS TO MOVE

- PROPERTY VALUES ARE DECREASING OR HAVE STAGNATED in your neighborhood, so you are unlikely to recover at least 80 percent of remodeling costs.
- THE LOCATION NO LONGER MEETS YOUR NEEDS, as happens when the kids move out and you'd prefer to live closer to downtown.
- YOUR CURRENT HOUSE IS A LOT DIFFERENT FROM THE HOUSE YOU REALLY WANT. You might be living in a ranch house but have always pined for a three-story brownstone.

REASONS TO REMODEL

- WITH A FEW MODIFICATIONS, YOUR HOUSE WOULD BE JUST PERFECT. A house with a comfortable layout and sound structure has "good bones" and thus can be an ideal candidate for remodeling.
- YOURS IS THE UGLIEST HOUSE ON THE BLOCK. Congratulations— bringing a humble house up to neighborhood standards is one of the few sure ways to make money in remodeling.
- IT'S HARD TO PART WITH MATURE TREES, CLOSE FRIENDS, AND A CONVENIENT LOCATION. Since almost any house can be modified to better suit your needs and wants, disregard all the above advice in "Reasons to Move" if you're lucky enough to have found the best address on earth for you.

a major project. Before drafting blueprints, driving a nail, or dunking a brush, take a long, hard look at whether remodeling can give you what you want—or whether you might be better off moving.

The good news about remodeling is that, potentially, you can accomplish almost anything. In my 30 years as a remodeling contractor, I have restored houses condemned to demolition, added thousands of square feet where it seemed you couldn't append an inch, and turned drab digs into designer dwellings. The bad news is that remodeling does not always make good economic sense.

For example, if you want a five-bedroom, 4,500-sq.-ft. house, but the largest home in your neighborhood is only 2,500 sq. ft. with three bedrooms, there's a good chance you will never recover your investment. Likewise, remodeling won't shorten your commute to work, improve your schools, or make your neighbors more neighborly. Unless you love your area and the local housing market clearly allows you to upgrade your home without turning it into the priciest property on the block, you should pause for a deep breath and then consult a real estate agent or an appraiser before remodeling.

These professionals can be helpful even if you feel sure that remodeling makes financial sense, because it's good to know the limits of your local real estate market. Their advice will probably confirm the wisdom of approaching your project with a sharp pencil and an unblinking eye on the budget.

It's also possible to err on the side of being too frugal. Cheap products and low bids often result in poor performance and reduced durability. If you're going through all the

A thin plastic base plated with chrome makes this $10 faucet look like metal, but it won't last long if you plan to use daily—certainly not long enough to justify replacement.

This Moen® faucet (model L4720) looks more expensive than it is at about $60, but will last ten or fifteen years, making it more affordable in the long run than a cheap faucet.

THE TENDENCY TO OVERIMPROVE

Once you've lived in a house a while, you develop a dream of what the place could become. And realizing the dream might just price your home well above the other properties in the neighborhood. To constrain your remodeling plans, try photographing average-looking houses within a two-block radius and compare your house to these shots. Instead of investing in dressing up the place, make changes on the inside that will improve your everyday comfort and pleasure.

REMODELING IS BIG BUSINESS

Remodeling accounts for about 2 percent of the nation's economic activity and 40 percent of total residential investment. In total dollar volume per year, remodeling outpaces commercial construction or public works construction. What was a $200-billion industry in 2003 is projected to reach $213 billion by 2010.

trouble of remodeling, you don't want to have to sell your house a few years from now as a fixer-upper with frayed carpets, windows that don't work, and peeling paint. Here's the unavoidable truth: It's always more expensive to do the job twice. In the following chapters, you will learn how to save money intelligently, without compromising on quality or aesthetics. In the building trades we call this approach "optimum value engineering," which is just industry jargon for saying you should weigh your goals against your options and then apply common sense to get the biggest bang for your construction buck.

To squeeze full value from every remodeling dollar, you've got to make wise choices in materials and construction methods, then learn how to economically reproduce the aesthetic essence of high-end finishes. These twin themes—optimum value engineering and affordably creating million-dollar details—represent the heart of this book. It's a practical, financially responsible approach that can be applied to remodeling projects at

WHETHER YOU DO IT YOURSELF OR HIRE A GENERAL CONTRACTOR, you can always save money by maintaining control of the design, scope of work, and materials.

Before you commit to a major reworking of your home, be sure to anticipate the disruption to your household and your life. It's all too easy to focus on the finished product and forget about the messy process.

any price point, from modest to magnificent. To carry it out, you'll need to spend time researching and planning; in return, you'll spend far less money.

Why Remodel?

Why bother with the stress, mess, and expense of remodeling? For one, consider the money you can save by staying put rather than buying a new home. Selling and moving expenses represent about 10 percent of the value of a house. Add to this the cost of new furnishings and the chaos of relocating,

and suddenly an intelligent remodeling plan starts to make a lot of sense.

There are other advantages to reworking your present address. In most municipalities, buying a new house will nudge you into higher property taxes, possibly including special assessments negotiated by the developer with the municipality. You can upgrade your existing house substantially without increasing your property taxes if you don't add square footage. But the principal advantage of remodeling over moving is that you can put the thousands you've saved on relocation into tangible assets. You may find that you can get a lot closer to your dream house by improving instead of moving.

Time Is Not Money

Remodeling always takes a lot longer than your original guesstimate. And affordable remodeling requires more time because you have to become a fastidious planner. You'll want to think through every detail and write it down. Once construction begins, it's easy to get carried away and spend more money than you ever dreamed. Some contractors will actually bid a job at cost on the theory that they will earn a handsome profit on changes, thanks to all the details the homeowner forgot.

Impulse buying is the biggest budget pitfall. Never make a snap decision under pressure. The slow and thoughtful approach provides the best safeguard against reckless spending. Unfortunately, even with diligent planning and careful budgeting, every remodeling project represents a big outlay. It's also a disruption. A disassembled house can become a frustrating living environment after a month or two. And once you've started, you can't quit. One way to cope with washing dishes in the bathtub and eating takeout every night is to turn the job into an adventure. With a can-do attitude that turns roughing it into family fun, you can save a bundle by contracting the work yourself.

Or, if you don't like takeout and decide to hire a contractor to complete the job while you vacation in Tahiti, you still should plan and budget with care. Losing control of a remodeling project is like loosening the reins on a wild stallion: Costs will run wild. By becoming personally familiar with each phase of the project, you will end up with the house you want. Just be prepared for the process to take a little—or a lot—longer than it might have if you turned over all the decisions to the people you hire.

START BY DREAMING

Homeowners tend to think the first stage in a remodeling project is drawing up plans or making a budget. But before addressing these practical matters, you need to know what you want to accomplish, and that means allowing yourself to dream.

Your satisfaction with any remodeling project depends on how closely you can approximate your ideal living environment. This ideal corresponds to two attributes, one practical and the other emotional. On the practical side, you need comfort, safety, and enough room to work and play contentedly. The emotional side has to do with the feeling you want to come home to, as well as the "look" that makes you want to host a party.

To help focus on how you'd like your home to look and function, organize a planning notebook. You'll need a thick three-ring binder with 15 or more tabbed dividers. Label the tabs with the rooms in your house, such as *mudroom, bedroom,* and *kitchen,* then stock these sections with lined or graph paper. Add trade-specific labels, such as *cabinets, flooring, windows, appliances,* and *light fixtures.* Invest in a high-quality three-hole punch. As you find magazine articles or photos that appeal to you, clip and file them in the corresponding sections of the binder.

Program Statement: Put It into Words

Next, with the notebook in hand, come up with what architects call a *program statement.* This is the process in which you sort out your needs by listing your current home's shortcomings and possible remedies. Visit each room in turn and jot down what you would like to change. How do you imagine these spaces to look, work, and feel?

For now, just record your dreams and discontents. For example, you might write: "I'm tired of walking down two flights to the laundry room. I need more space to fold clothes. I would like the laundry area to feel spacious, airy, and bright." It might be that the kitchen doesn't seem large and gracious enough for entertaining. Or you might need another bathroom. Perhaps it would be nice to have a king-size bed, but the master bedroom is too small to accommodate one.

An idea note book will help you define a remodeling project and communicate your concept to contractors and designers.

IF YOU HAVE KIDS AT HOME, CONSIDER HOW OLD THEY WILL BE WHEN YOU FINISH YOUR REMODELING PROJECT. For example, if a child soon will be leaving home, you might consider robbing a few square feet from his or her bedroom to make a larger master bath in which you could install a shower seat or soaking tub.

After the cabinets, windows, and appliances went in, the owners of this kitchen had no money left for the accoutrements they wanted.

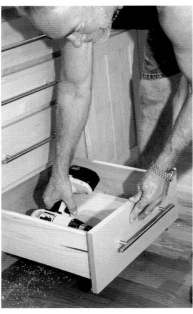

Within six months, they were able to add $750 worth of hardware.

Another six months later, they installed a $350 backsplash. Eventually, a $1,200 valance over the windows will add a splash of color and complete this progressive, four-stage kitchen remodel.

ALTHOUGH IMPULSE TO UPGRADE IS STRONG,
before plunging into adding cabinets and countertops,
remember to prioritize repairs.

PRO TIP

You might think it's silly to write down the obvious, but remodeling is a long process, and you can easily lose direction. The notebook will keep you in touch with your original intent. You'll be better able to gauge the authenticity of your decisions when the project runs into budget compromises, real estate realities, and other challenges. The notebook will also illustrate your vision for the architects, cabinetmakers, and contractors who eventually may collaborate with you. After 30 years in construction, I still use a three-ring binder with dividers to organize every project.

WORKING IN PHASES

You probably know someone whose home has been a remodeling zone for years. That doesn't have to be your fate if you break up the project into manageable segments. There are several ways to phase a home-improvement plan. You can break down remodeling into seasonal bites: spring, summer, fall, and winter projects. For example, late spring and early fall are the best times for exterior painting, siding, and roofing because daytime temperatures aren't as likely to be oppressive. Reserve heavy indoor remodeling jobs for the summer months, when it's too hot to work outside. Cosmetic work, such as interior painting, adding trim, and installing accessories, are wonderful winter pastimes.

You also can phase remodeling by work areas, dividing your project into architectural segments to tackle one at a time. This summer you might remove a dining-room wall to expand the kitchen, install hardwood floors, and finish up with a fresh coat of paint. A

year later, you could remodel the kitchen by replacing counters, adding an island, and installing new appliances. Wait another year before installing kitchen cabinet hardware, a tiled backsplash, and accent colors.

Setting Priorities

Still another way to organize your remodeling plan is to classify your projects as *repair, refurbishing,* or *remodeling.* Although repairs lack "sex appeal," they should always come first, especially when they involve leaks.

PRIORITIZE HOME REPAIRS

Putting a list of home repairs in order of importance can be a matter of personal safety as well as a way of making the best use of your time and money.

SAFETY FIRST. Fix or replace broken railings, loose steps, cracked plugs, and other household hazards.

FIX LEAKS. Water damage can be insidious, taking place out of sight. Replace the roof or patch cracks in the foundation before completing cosmetic repairs.

UPDATE SYSTEMS. Old electrical wiring, furnaces, and water heaters consume excessive energy and can pose fire hazards. Have these systems checked and, if necessary, update them.

SEAL CRACKS. Caulking around windows and doors, insulating attics, and replacing weatherstripping won't constitute a beauty makeover for your home, but they are the most cost-effective home-improvement projects you'll ever do. Each dollar spent on carefully applied expanding foam sealant and caulk can potentially save you $100 the next winter.

It's tempting to get straight to work on adding attractive upgrades, but most remodeling projects begin with at least a few humble repairs.

Water can damage a house quickly and critically, escalating costs as damp areas mildew and deteriorate. Avoid safety hazards, such as a wobbly banister or frayed wiring, by moving repairs to the top of your list—ahead of rose granite counters and Italian marble tile. To determine what repairs should be tackled first, hire a professional home inspector to advise you on the seriousness of any damage. This way, you won't be surprised by budget-busting bad news, such as having to replace a water heater, later on during remodeling

Items in the category of refurbishing come right after repair. These projects include cleaning, painting, and otherwise renewing old surfaces. Achieving your ends with paint, new flooring, and a fancy light fixture or two is the most affordable approach. A kitchen with new countertops, accent colors, and hardware can feel pristine at little expense. Because your dollars stretch farther when

spent on refurbishing, you may find it cost effective to allot at least 80 percent of your budget to fixing worn surfaces and the rest to remodeling. Some real estate speculators have become wealthy buying old, shabby houses and then flipping them for a profit after completing only cosmetic upgrades. Never underestimate the power of paint.

Remodeling costs more than cosmetic upgrades because it means more work. You may find that remodeling becomes necessary when your house no longer accommodates your lifestyle as your family grows, or when traditional rooms no longer serve your needs. In older homes, for example, kitchens were places to cook, not entertain. Closets were big enough for only a few garments. Rooms felt confining by today's standards.

Although size matters in real estate, it's more important to consider how useful the square footage: A 2,000-sq.-ft. house with 400 sq. ft. devoted to halls is effectively

This dated kitchen, (facing page), was in obvious need of improvements, but the owner lacked the money to carry out an extensive remodeling.

The low-cost transformation was accomplished with little more than contemporary plastic laminate, accent paint, and a new range.

Staying within the Envelope

Remodeling within the envelope of your existing home will cost less than constructing an addition. The savings can be spent on a higher quality of materials, finishes, and workmanship.

Existing home
- Yard left intact
- Living space added within footprint
- Money spent on better materials and finishes rather than on structure

Site work is disruptive, involves landscaping
- New foundation requires excavation
- New walls and roof add greatly to cost
- Larger footprint means higher taxes

WHEN HIRING A TRADESPERSON, TRUST YOUR INTUITION.
If you don't care for an individual—even if you can't put your finger
on just why—then keep looking for someone else, even if you like
the quoted price.

TRADE SECRET SELECTING SUBS

When you act as your own general contractor, your
subcontractors become your hands, eyes, and advisers,
so it's crucial to assemble a good team. Once you find
a tradesperson you like to work with, ask him or her
for referrals in other areas of construction. If you can
hire subcontractors who know and respect each other,
your project will start to coordinate itself, as if you had
hired a team of magical elves. On the other hand, if you
hire people who don't get along, you'll feel like a police
officer trying to keep the peace. You'll also spend a lot
of time on the phone lobbying the various subcontractors to show up and finish the job. Remember that the
best tool you have for persuasion is your signature on a
check. Never pay for work that has not been completed,
and never cut the last check until you're sure the job is
satisfactory.

smaller than a 1,800-sq.-ft. floor plan with
100 sq. ft. of halls. In essence, remodeling is
"adding on" without incurring the cost of
building beyond the home's envelope, avoid-
ing the big expenses of constructing foundations, exterior walls, and a roof.

Phasing Spares Your Nerves and Budget

By phasing and prioritizing your remodeling projects, you take the anxiety out of the
work left pending. When we moved into
our house, we had a huge list of improvements to complete, including landscaping,
finishing the basement, and remodeling
the master closet. The list seemed endless,
urgent, and impossible to complete until I
remembered my own advice. I made a list,
prioritized items, set up four seasonal phases
to complete the projects, and got to work. At
the end of that first day, having planted several trees, I felt stress free and in control. The
unfinished basement didn't faze me because
I knew that particular task was scheduled for
the fall.

Finally, working in prioritized phases can
spread out the expense of a large undertaking over time. This becomes especially
important if you expand the scope of your
remodel as great ideas pop into your head in
the middle of construction.

DO IT YOURSELF OR HIRE IT OUT?

As you develop your plan, it helps to think
in terms of three levels of owner involve-
ment: doing most of the work yourself,

APPLIANCE AND PLUMBING MANUFACTURERS ADD ON ALL SORTS OF EXTRA FEATURES, hoping to snare more customers. By isolating your (real) needs, you may be able to find an unadvertised, low-cost alternative that will save you money.

doing some of the work and hiring subcontractors to do the rest, and engaging a general contractor to handle everything from coordinating construction to fixing a price and then guaranteeing the results.

Few of us can or want to do all of the work ourselves. But even if you turn over the majority of the remodeling to a qualified contractor, you may choose to perform tasks such as moving furniture and cleaning that will allow you to save money while not interfering with the work. In deciding what to take on, you'll want to consider how much skill, time, and interest you bring to a project. For example, if you like working with your hands but never handled a saw, skip difficult jobs and instead install things like towel bars and ceiling fans.

DIY

The more work you do, the less you'll spend. DIY (doing it yourself) takes longer to finish, and if you don't have a lot of skill and practice, the results might be less than satisfactory. Keep in mind that some of the simplest trades to understand, such as bricklaying, require years to master. Nevertheless, if spending a Saturday afternoon framing a wall is your idea of fulfillment, then you stand to gain a very tangible sense of achievement along with the monetary savings.

Contracting It Yourself

The middle ground is acting as your own general contractor. You coordinate the subcontractors and do some of the work yourself, such as demolition, light framing, and patching and painting. Leave the heavy

NAILING DOWN THE SPECS & SCOPE

In determining the materials you want for your project, it's important to take care with the specifications, or *specs*. For example, the phrase "Hem fir 2x4s at 24 in. on center" describes a type of lumber and its spacing within a framed wall. "Koehler® bathtub number 515 in white" describes a particular product that you've selected. The more complete and precise your specifications, the more tightly you can control the budget—and the products that end up in your home.

When dealing with a contractor, it's also important to deal with the *scope* of the project—the extent of the work and services you expect. You might want the job done within a week, with cleanup carried out on a daily basis. But unless you review the scope of the work with your contractor, disagreements and disappointments are apt to result.

lifting and technical trades to the experts. By hiring electricians, plumbers, and finish carpenters without the services of a general contractor, you can save about 30 percent.

If your project involves only one trade, such as roofing, or a handful of trades without overlap, such as roofing, painting, and flooring, you should hire these professionals yourself rather than working through a general contractor. Negotiating with a painter or carpet installer isn't so difficult that you need professional intermediation. Just read the corresponding trade section in this book, search for the products you want to use, and ask the supplier for a referral. Talk to several installers for suggestions and prices, then

PRO TIP

BRING A CONTRACTOR INTO THE PROCESS EARLY ON, when you're developing a design and coming up with a budget. In effect, you'll have the services of a professional cost consultant who can make suggestions on keeping your project affordable.

QUIZZING THE CONTRACTOR

Here's a list of questions to weave into the conversation when interviewing prospective remodeling contractors.

- Does the contractor belong to trade organizations such as the National Association of the Remodeling Industry or business groups such as the Better Business Bureau? Serious builders usually are affiliated with industry organizations.
- Does the contractor specialize in remodeling projects, with jobs similar to yours?
- Ask if the contractor works alone, with employees, or only through subcontractors. A contractor with employees and subs can more easily complete a job quickly and pay wages commensurate with the tasks involved. You don't want a $60-an-hour carpenter hauling lumber and cleaning up.
- Ask how many jobs the contractor has concurrently and how your project fits into the schedule. Good contractors usually stay busy, but they should be able to provide a realistic idea of their availability.
- Will the job be supervised by the contractor or by a superintendent? If the subcontractors will be allowed to run the project, then you might as well act as your own general and save the fee.
- Ask for a written schedule before starting work.
- Ask if you can visit a current job to interview the owner and see how the job site looks. If the job is a mess and the owner looks frazzled—well, you get the picture.

choose the one that combines a reasonable price, good references, and a personality that makes you feel comfortable.

By acting as your own contractor, you also can shop around and find the best prices, whereas a general contractor isn't likely to take the time to comparison shop. For example, who says you have to buy all of your light fixtures or appliances from one supplier? Instead, make a list of items you need along with three columns in which to note the cost of each at three different stores. Highlight the lowest price in each category, and you've got yourself a shopping list.

You should know that the construction business revolves around relationships. A good general contractor comes with a cadre of loyal subcontractors who have agreed to work to his or her price and scheduling requirements. Subcontractors have an incentive to provide lower costs and reliable service to someone who hires them repeatedly. You, on the other hand, lack that advantage, and your budget may give way if subcontractors charge you full price. Your schedule may slip, too, when subcontractors put familiar employers ahead of you.

Don't lose faith. Given time (and good referrals), you can find tradespeople who charge an affordable price, show up on time, and even offer advice on your project. Remember that although general contractors can often negotiate a lower price, they make money by reselling the service at retail. A contractor's fee averages 30 percent, even if your bill shows only 15 percent or 20 percent, with the balance made up by the markup over wholesale prices.

Hiring a Contractor

If all this sounds like more work than it's worth, or if your project is large enough to require professional coordination, find a reputable general contractor. Contractors affiliated with remodeling industry groups, such as the National Association of Home Builders (NAHB) and the National Association of the Remodeling Industry (NARI), have professional certifications, subscribe to a code of ethics, and engage in continuing education to keep up to date. These contractors follow good business practices, but they won't necessarily do so within your budget.

You've heard that it's wise to get three competitive bids, but unless you have an ironclad set of specifications and plans, you will receive bids across the board and end up hiring the contractor who omitted the most items from the estimate. Instead, *interview* at least three reputable remodeling contractors. Choose the one who best understands your needs, offers to help you meet your budget targets, and seems like a person you'll be able to get along with over the months to come.

BALANCING THE BUDGET

Two things determine your budget: how much money you *can* spend on remodeling and how much you *need* to spend to get the job done. Your upper limit depends on three factors: how much money you have, the value of real estate in your area, and your priorities.

If you have $20,000 in cash and can borrow $80,000 on a home equity loan, your ceiling is $100,000. On the other hand, if the most expensive houses in your area don't exceed $300,000, and you live in a house that cost you $250,000, you probably shouldn't invest more in remodeling than the house will be worth on the market, especially if you plan to move in two or three years. On the other hand, if you love the neighborhood and plan to stay put for a decade or more, this strictly monetary consideration becomes less important.

Developing a Preliminary Estimate

Once your plans begin to take shape, you're ready to create a preliminary cost estimate. In addition to talking with subcontractors, you can buy a remodeling cost manual that contractors use to appraise projects (home centers carry them). Although the only estimates that really count are the bids you will eventually get, these books can help you develop a realistic cost basis for planning your project.

Cost manuals use several approaches to price jobs. The simplest and least accurate is the square foot method. Unfortunately, this is also the most common method. A statement like "remodeling costs $150 to $250 a square foot" means little, given the range of possibilities. A more accurate estimate breaks the project down into smaller components. Instead of trying to appraise all of the job costs simultaneously, you break the job down by operation. Let's say you want to frame a wall that's 8 ft. high and runs 12 ft. The job will include installing two electrical outlets, hanging and finishing drywall on both sides, painting the room, and installing carpet. Once you have the figures for every aspect (framing, electrical, drywall, paint, and carpet), you can refer to the cost guide manual to arrive at an accurate estimate.

For help in coming up with a budget, consult the remodeling cost books sold at lumber-yards, home centers, and bookstores. You'll find costs for everything from removing a countertop to installing a residential elevator. Some guides are published in software form, making it easier to scroll through items and keep track of the math.

Vinyl windows are least expensive, and come in almost every sash configuration, with internally glazed mullions and excellent energy-efficient designs (see chapter 5).

Using drywall detailing and paint-grade medium density fiberboard moldings you can achieve the same, old-world opulence while trimming the budget (see chapter 6).

This sunny dining room might inspire you to remodel, but the large windows, elaborate wood trim, bead-board wainscoting, and rich wood flooring might push you over budget.

At about a third less the price of wood flooring, plastic laminate flooring comes in almost limitless wood-tone variety (see chapter 6).

A talented designer can earn his or her fee by helping you arrive at coordinated aesthetic choices while spending within your means.

The biggest estimating errors are caused by omission, not miscalculation. By scrolling through the endless lists of itemized components in a cost guide, you are less likely to forget something. It's common for a contractor to score a job as the low bidder and then realize he or she overlooked something—say, 2,000 sq. ft. of roofing. This won't happen if you go through several iterations of the construction cost estimate. In the end, you will know your costs by heart. As you study the manual, you will notice that costs are broken down for labor, materials, equipment, and a markup. *Labor* often is the highest, especially for demolition, painting, and cleanup. These are projects in which a do-it-yourselfer can save real money. If *materials* represent half the cost or more, you can save by studying alternative products and specifying the best

value in materials. *Equipment* rarely becomes a big-ticket item in remodeling, but if you take on jobs that require special tools (such as floor sanding and blow-in insulation), you may find that the cost of materials and tool rental cancel out the DIY advantages. By studying the overhead and profit column as well, you can get an idea of how much you can save by parsing the project down into smaller components and carrying out the work yourself.

When you hire a subcontractor to take care of materials, labor, equipment, and supervision, you pay a *markup* for every part of the project. And if you add a general contractor to the mix, there will be a further markup. But for the added expense, you receive cost and quality guarantees along with experienced project management. Building is a risky business that involves thousands of parts and dozens of people. Anyone in the trade will tell you that builders earn their pay. Still, if you're willing to take on some of the work of bidding, hiring, purchasing, cleanup, and oversight, then you should earn a profit, too.

Purchasing Materials

There's something I call the Goldilocks principle: Never buy too cheap, and never buy too expensive. Cheap products can fail prematurely and double your replacement costs. Expensive items generally come loaded with useless upgrades that do not necessarily improve reliability. For example, a dishwasher with lots of options is apt to

CONSULT WITH YOUR TAX ADVISER if your remodeling project includes upgrading insulation, windows, lighting, and heating and air-conditioning equipment, or adding alternative-energy products. You may qualify for tax credits that help offset the cost of construction.

PRO TIP

run less efficiently and break down more frequently while probably not doing a better job of washing the dishes. Many manufacturers carry a builder's or professional line that combines lower cost with long-term reliability. This standard usually will match your needs.

GREEN REMODELING

You don't drive a Ford℠ Model T™, but chances are you live in one. The home-building industry has been slow to pick up on technological innovations that use fewer materials and less energy. A trend called *green building* is changing that. In the chapters that follow, you will learn about some of these techniques. Some builders and homeowners won't try these new methods because they equate time-honored practices with higher quality. But just as the old-school approach isn't better when it comes to computers and airplanes, it also isn't better when it comes to houses.

Also, overbuilding structural systems will not ensure higher quality. I use every new technology described in this book by preference. Each has universal code approval, backed by years of industry and university research. They are your means to saving money over traditional construction.

Energy Offsets

Although you want to remodel frugally, you also should factor in the long-term expense of maintenance and operation. For example,

if you install slightly more expensive windows with a low U-value (an indication of the window's insulation properties), you might eventually recover the added cost and even save money in energy savings. In other words, consider the cost of a product over the period you expect to occupy your house in order to get a true idea of your least expensive option. As with buying a discounted gas-guzzling automobile, choosing an inexpensive and inefficient building material may cost you more in the long run.

This does not mean that every product that touts energy efficiency is a good buy. Some, such as super high-efficiency heat pumps, can take longer to pay off in energy savings than the product will last. When shopping around, ask for an estimate of how much money you will save annually. As a rule, if it takes 6 years or less to pay off the difference and the product's lifespan is at least 15 years, the investment is a wise one.

While high-end water heaters and air-conditioners may not save you money, low-tech green building technologies and energy-saving construction methods can pay handsome dividends. For example, a tight house allows you to reduce the size of your heating and air-conditioning equipment so that you save on first costs as well as on long-term operation. Remember that, while new does not always equal improved, manufacturers have worked hard to solve problems of energy efficiency, indoor air quality, and durability, which are manifest in countless new products.

This tub is a foot longer than most, allowing you to stretch out and luxuriate, and because it doesn't create bubbles, the cost is only about half that of a cheap whirlpool.

2

Blueprint to Affordability

ARCHITECTS ARE IN THE BUSINESS of transforming dreams into drawings. This chapter shows how you can use your own plans and sketches in the same way to realize the changes you want to make. You don't need drafting skills or a T-square, just graph paper to keep things to scale, tracing paper to revise your ideas easily, and a tape measure to plot your home's existing features and to eyeball the size of possible alterations.

The remodeling process begins with identifying the things you'd like to change or replace, as described in chapter 1. From there, you work through a series of rough sketches and floor plans to arrive at the working drawings that will guide construction. By progressing in stages, you can dream freely on paper before committing yourself to hard-cost construction.

The builders of this house didn't take advantage of the mountain and lake views. The remodelers took the unusual step of installing a picture window in a bathroom.

Photo courtesy of SawHorse Construction, Atlanta, Ga.

SITE ANALYSIS: LOOKING AT WHERE YOU LIVE

The first step in almost all architectural projects involves considering how the building relates to the property. It might not seem you'd need to bother with this *site analysis* step for a remodeling project, because you're not figuring out where to build on vacant land. Nevertheless, it pays to take a critical look at how your home sits on the lot. That's especially true if you live in a tract house, because builders have stock plans that they tend to reuse without much regard for individual lot characteristics.

A walk around your house may reveal opportunities: a potential good view or a weed-choked side yard that could become a garden courtyard with a French door opening onto it from a newly remodeled kitchen. Nothing adds value and enjoyment at a lower price than taking advantage of what's already there.

SCHEMATIC DRAWINGS: THINKING ALOUD ON PAPER

Next, start exploring the possibilities inside your house. *Schematic drawings* are where the excitement begins. Architects usually sketch

Thinking on Paper

You can draw freehand floor plans as a way of exploring possibilities. The before-and-after sketches shown here were done by SawHorse Construction, in Atlanta, to conceptualize a bathroom remodel. Even the most sophisticated designs start with rough sketches.

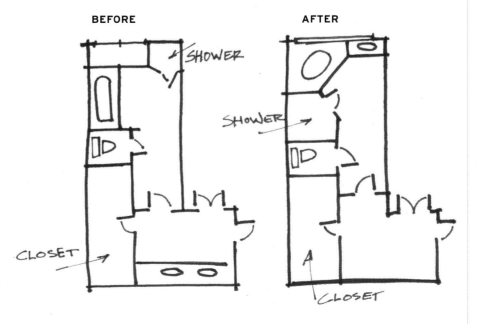

When sketching your floor plan on graph paper, a convenient scale is to have each square on the sheet represent 1 ft. Begin by drawing the perimeter of the house, using the dimensions you get by going outside with a tape measure. Back inside the house, measure to locate the interior walls, doors, and windows on your drawing. You don't have to be perfectly accurate at this stage; a good representation will do. Photocopy this plan to allow experimenting with various layouts. It's also a good idea to have tracing paper on hand so that you can try out different ideas. (If you have a particularly complicated floor plan or an especially large house, consider hiring a drafting service to create and reproduce the floor plan at ¼-in. scale.)

TRADE SECRET
DEFINE WITHOUT DIVISION

If you want a solid, permanent separation between rooms, consider a 6-ft.-high wall that divides without entirely closing off adjoining spaces. Short walls also work well for a closet, laundry room, or foyer. In most cases, it's not necessary to cap these with a low ceiling, which would only add expense and become a dust trap. The low walls not only enhance the sense of space but also permit the free flow of air, reducing the need for ducts. In areas requiring fire sprinklers, these partial walls may make it unnecessary to go to the expense of adding sprinkler heads.

them freehand in multiple generations, elaborating their ideas until they look and feel right. Several architects may work on a variety of alternatives; likewise, it's a good idea to include different points of view in the initial stages of your design, such as from a spouse or partner.

Floor Plans: A Bird's-Eye View

To hone your design ideas, start with a scale drawing of your existing house, or at least the parts you want to modify. No matter how well you think you know your home, the bird's-eye view offered by a floor plan reveals spatial relationships that are difficult to notice without seeing everything at once. For example, you might spot the potential to enlarge a bathroom by robbing a few feet from the linen closet, or to expand the kitchen by knocking down the dining-room wall. It also might occur to you to switch the functions of a room, such as creating a first-floor master-bedroom suite in what's now the living room.

You'll find it easier to think creatively about alternative room uses if you hold off labeling the rooms. (You might want to identify rooms with existing plumbing, however, because it can be expensive and inconvenient to relocate supply and drain

Uncover the skeleton of an old house, and you are likely to find that framing members tended to be beefy and rough-hewn, rather than conforming to today's stock lumber dimensions. Old construction also may not meet modern structural requirements. Notice that this window, in a bearing wall, has no structural header.

The window now adds a strong architectural element, and the angled ceilings create visual interest.

AFTER

BEFORE

The architectural possibilities of this attic might not strike you immediately. The window dormer looks small and tunnel-like, and the walls are low and cramped. But a little creative remodeling can turn a forgotten space under the eaves into a favorite retreat.

TRADE SECRET HOW TO IDENTIFY A BEARING WALL

Before you consider removing or altering an interior wall, determine if it is weight bearing. A number of clues will suggest this is the case:

■ The wall runs perpendicular to the joists.

■ The wall is near the center of the house or a large span.

■ The ceiling joists meet and overlap over the wall.

■ The wall has plywood or OSB (oriented strand board) sheathing.

■ The wall incorporates posts or large headers.

You still may be unsure at this point. If so, determine the size of the joists that span the distance on either side of the wall and consult a span table to see if they are sufficient to go this total distance without intermediate support. If they are not, then the wall at midspan must be bearing.

To fully exploit the space within the existing walls of your home, consider reclaiming unused chases and tucking art nooks into walls, such as the space here that accommodates a single water pipe.

lines.) For now, view each room as a shape with limitless potential. There is no reason that your current mudroom can't be your future laundry room, or that your coat closet can't become a powder room.

Having a floor plan of your existing house also facilitates discussing options with prospective designers and contractors. They'll more easily grasp your vision if you illustrate it on paper than if you solely rely on words. And in the ensuing conversation, these professionals are likely to come up with changes that haven't occurred to you.

A floor plan may reveal ways to make your home seem larger without adding on. Consider the difference between cooking in a cramped 10-ft. by 15-ft. kitchen and entertaining in an adjacent 10-ft. by 10-ft. dining room, or doing both in a combined kitchen/dining room that includes an island and a large table.

Don't forget to sketch the "dead areas" too, such as the attic, a seldom-visited back porch, storage rooms, and under-stair space. You may hit upon novel ways of incorporating them into your remodeling scheme. At a minimum, you can take advantage of dead spaces by carving a whimsical art niche into the wall, building in recessed shelves, or adding a nook for hanging coats. In other words, explore your house without preconceptions.

DON'T FORGET TO CONSIDER THE WATER-HEATER CLOSET in your list of areas for potential expansion. You could switch to an on-demand water heater, freeing up the space taken by the bulky tank of a standard unit.

BEFORE

Faced with a dark and dreary living room, my firm removed about 50 sq. ft. of floor to bring in light and enlarge the interior vista. The house feels bigger, even though it lost a bit of floor area in the process.

AFTER

Next, place tracing paper over your original floor plan and outline the exterior walls and any interior *bearing walls* with a felt-tipped pen. These walls support the weight of the roof or the floors above and are more expensive to remove or modify, so try to reconfigure without altering them. Next, trace every other wall in the house with pencil and consider these as flexible fixtures that you can eliminate or reposition at will.

Less Is More: Using Both Ends of the Pencil

At this stage, your remodeling is just a drawing. You can change your mind a thousand times without charge, so be bold. The most

GET THE ARCHITECTURE RIGHT FIRST. Your floor plan and elevations represent the cake; designer details are the icing. Remain authentic in style and consistent in scale. Good taste always looks more expensive—and usually costs less.

The New Math: Adding by Subtraction

Notice how walls were removed to create a bigger feel and better flow in this kitchen/dining-room remodel. Instead of chopping up the area with walls and counters, the new layout defines areas of activity with an island and wide connecting passageways, resulting in a spacious family-friendly environment.

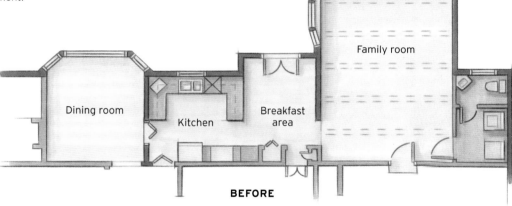

BEFORE

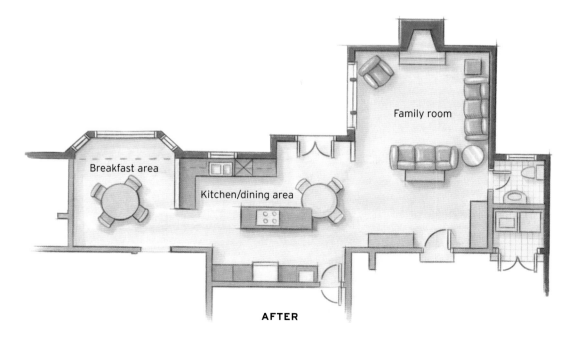

AFTER

Although removing a bearing wall entails the structural step of adding a header, the resulting opening can dramatically integrate a home's floor plan, as was the case with this kitchen.

AFTER

DURING

BEFORE

economical end of a pencil is the eraser. Instead of enlarging by *addition,* consider ways of creating space by *subtraction.* Remove non-bearing walls to combine small rooms into larger, loftlike multipurpose areas. Floors can be erased, as well. In a two-story house, you might remove a few square feet of the second floor to allow light to bathe the lower floor and create longer sight lines that improve the visual interaction between levels.

Enlarging through subtraction works especially well in small, older homes with a front-to-back string of small, use-specific rooms such as a parlor followed by a living room, dining room, kitchen, and back porch. This shotgun style, designed to shoe-horn houses on narrow city lots, is a layout that's easy to walk through but difficult to live in. Nowadays, architects create comfort

even in small spaces by blending rooms into large, inviting places.

Homes are less likely to feel confining when activities, instead of walls, define the rooms. This doesn't mean you have to live in an amphitheater. You can create definition by varying ceiling heights, wall textures, even flooring. Most rooms do not require hard divisions, just a soft delineation of space in a way that creates intimacy. By using design elements instead of walls to separate areas of activity, your house becomes flexible. And with improved flow, it will seem larger.

When searching for ways to combine rooms, look first to those you use least. If your dining room comes in handy only twice a year, during turkey and tax

If you're going to cut back on the partitions that carve up a small house, skimp on closets. An armoire holds enough clothing and linens for a guest or child's room.

Within a very small space, this loft condominium remodel takes advantage of low walls and a raised floor to differentiate the dining area from the living room. An added bonus is the pull-out futon bed that slips under the floor, doubling as a love seat when retracted.

seasons, it might be a candidate for assimilation. Although doing away with the dining room diminishes the elegance of a formal dinner, many families find they enjoy the effects of removing a wall and incorporating the dining room into the kitchen or family room. Likewise, if you rarely socialize in the living room, consider converting it into a comfortable family room.

Floor plans that are chopped up by lots of walls often reflect bygone sensibilities. If your kitchen feels isolated, remove the door, make the opening a few inches wider, and open it all the way to the ceiling. The kitchen will feel more welcoming. Have a small master bedroom and bathroom? Remove one bathroom wall, pull the vanity sinks into the bedroom, and add a wall to separate bathtub and toilet. You'll have a larger-feeling bedroom and bathroom, as shown in chapter 7, "Affordable Kitchens & Baths" (beginning on p. 160).

Structural Savvy

Erasing walls is easy on paper and even easy enough in real life—if you're not tearing down bearing walls. Removing these structural elements entails finding a new path to transfer the load from above down to the foundation. We explore how to do that in the next chapter, but before you choose that relatively complex option, consider adding an opening instead.

You usually can span openings up to 6 ft. wide with a standard wood *header*, as the top framing member of the opening is termed. A lumberyard or contractor can determine the appropriate header size using a table that

Photo by Ken Gutmekar

A bearing wall once separated these two rooms. Notice how the columns open the space while providing an appealing line of definition.

calculates the type of beam needed to carry a given load, such as a 4-ft. opening carrying the floor or roof above. You also can replace the bearing wall with columns, which can serve as decorative features that suit the décor of the home. Structurally, columns work by breaking a long span into shorter ones so that smaller beams carry the load. Columns also provide opportunities for "soft" separation of rooms, in which these structural elements are integrated into bookshelves or cabinets.

Planning around Your Plumbing

Your remodeling plans are likely to include adding or altering a bathroom or kitchen.

Unaltered from its original configuration, this window preserves the structure and historic outline of the home.

The Making of a Master Bath

By reclaiming an adjacent closet, this bathroom was transformed into a true master bath
with a large shower, but the plumbing did not have to stray far from the existing sewer stack.

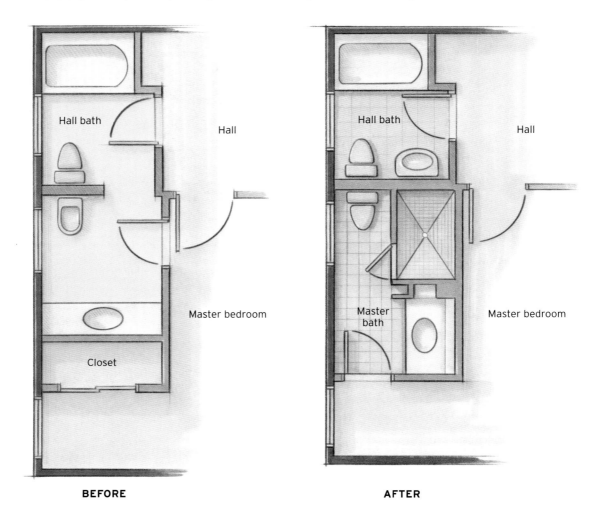

BEFORE

AFTER

If you want to add a bathroom, it's best to place the new fixtures on or near an existing plumbing location. Think of the home's plumbing system as a tree, with roots and branches. Although it is relatively easy to run water lines to a new location (branches), moving the sewer and ventilation lines (the trunk) can pose a serious challenge. This does not mean you have to live with the system as it is when remodeling a bathroom or kitchen; just keep in mind that the closer you stay to existing drain and vent lines, the less costly your project will be.

You might enlarge a bathroom by incorporating the adjacent linen closet or a portion of a walk-in closet, then compensate for the lost storage by adding a toilet topper or a kitchen pantry cabinet. Alternatively, place a pair of sinks in what had been the closet, making space in the existing bathroom for a toilet in its own niche and a luxurious shower. If enlarging the bathroom seems impractical, you can create the illusion of space by installing a floor-to-ceiling mirror, replacing a vanity with a pedestal sink, or adding a skylight to bathe the room with sunlight.

If you want to add a second-floor bath, consider carefully how the plumber will run drains to the existing *sewer stack* (a large vertical pipe into which horizontal lines run from sinks, toilets, and other fixtures). A large house might have more than one stack. To find a stack, locate the first-floor toilet plumbing and assume the stack rises in either the wall behind it or a nearby wall. Confirm the location by going down into the basement (or up in the attic if your house is on a slab) and looking for this large-diameter pipe. Once you find it, try to design your new bath at that location. Long horizontal drains are costly and sometimes difficult to install, especially if the new sewer line has to run through floor joists.

A plumber may be able to run new drain lines through existing walls or in boxed-out chases, though this complication always adds cost. Remember that drains have to run downhill, and long horizontal crossings can make drains sluggish and prone to clogs. Also, building codes require you to allow a certain clearance to the front and sides of sinks and toilets. To help ensure that you will arrive at an approved layout—and one that a plumber can build without much trouble—try tracing over a bathroom floor plan from a book or magazine and incorporating this layout into your design.

Kitchen plumbing may be somewhat more flexible, because a sink drain is narrower than a toilet drain. In two-story homes, however, moving the kitchen vent line is apt to cause problems because it runs from the sink through the roof. Try to place new sinks within 4 ft. to 6 ft. of the existing sink. Or use a special valve you'll learn about in chapter 4, which makes running vents out through the roof unnecessary.

Defining Space without Walls

After you have created space by erasing, you may want to define new areas, such as a sitting room, art nook, or study, though not necessarily by adding walls. To avoid the mistake of introducing pointless

The architect for my firm designed this study as a separate room, enclosed with four conventional walls. I used the footprint but built half-walls and a large, uncased opening to create a defined area that remained integrated with the floor plan.

A dramatic change in flooring defines this family room, separating it from the adjacent hall and dining room without creating a physical barrier.

AS YOU EXPERIMENT WITH LAYOUTS, keep in mind that people as well as furniture will occupy these rooms. For example, allow enough space around the dining-room table to allow for pulling out the chairs.

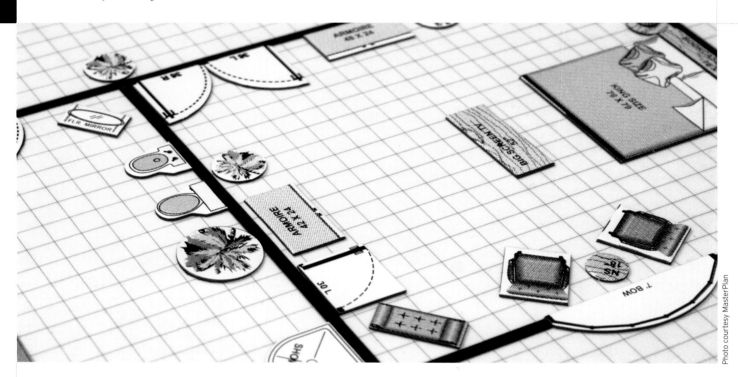

Photo courtesy MasterPlan

For a fully furnished reality check, use ¼-in.-scale furniture cutouts or magnetic pieces like these from Master-Plan Magnetics. This will give you a good idea of how spaces will work in real life—whether your dining-room table and chairs will fit comfortably in a remodeled space, for example. You'll also be able to explore ways of using furniture instead of walls to define rooms, reducing the need for new construction.

partitions, sketch in furniture to preview how these spaces may work. You might find that furniture can take the place of walls, inexpensively defining living areas without establishing architectural barriers that may suffocate a room or isolate it. Consider using other elements to delineate space, such as lighting, a lowered ceiling, a bay window, columns, a change in color and texture, or simply a throw rug.

To furnish your floor plan, go to a drafting supply store or search the Internet for a book of ¼-in.-scale furniture cutouts. These perforated sheets include most common household fixtures and appliances. You can also make your own scale-model cutouts by measuring the tables, sofas, and chairs you want to use and then reproducing them at ¼-in. scale as simple rectangles

and squares. Place these on the floor plan and see how well they create definition without walls.

Before drawing hard lines, try shading in areas where you might simply change finishes to revive your home's interior. I like to set one room off from the rest of the house by using an unusual texture on one wall, such as stucco, heavily textured wallpaper, or a veneer of furniture-grade plywood in maple, cherry, or birch. The less spent on studs and drywall, the more that's left for countertops and chandeliers. For example, you can suggest a barrier by matching a beam in the ceiling with a change in flooring material. Or you can transform the ambience of an area by adding indirect lighting to suggest a completely different environment with very little construction.

MATCH ROOM SIZES TO ACTIVITY. You may be able to gain the extra space you need by converting a room from one function to another, such as adding a chandelier in a corner of the living room for use as a dining area, freeing the dining room for other uses.

Walls, Partial and Movable

If you want to add walls to divide a large space into two separate rooms, there are affordable ways of doing it. By stopping the wall just 12 in. to 18 in. short of the ceiling, you can inexpensively establish a strong separation while adding light and a sense of spaciousness to both rooms. The gap also promotes the flow of air so there will be less need for additional ducts.

A screen-style room divider spares the expense of adding smoke detectors, switches, and outlets. Asian architects have used screens as room dividers for centuries, and modern versions might use whimsical mate-rials such as corrugated metals and Plexi-glas®. The effect is to add drama by inviting you to discover what lies beyond. Screens can carve out a private area, such as a guest room or reading nook, from a large com-mon space. This option is worth considering especially if one of the spaces is used only occasionally.

Reclaiming Unused Space

If you don't have enough living area, consider incorporating the garage, attic, sunroom, or basement. Reclaiming this space is a great way to add square feet at a fraction of the price of adding on.

This two-sided fireplace serves both as a focal point for the den and as a room divider to set off the dining area. The entertainment center is just a frame with doors, the interior work is done in drywall, and the wood is paint-grade poplar stained to look like cherry. The only relatively expensive ele-ment is the single band of cobalt-blue porcelain tile around the metal fireplace.

This breakfast nook was once a mudroom off the back porch. The owners reclaimed the space to enlarge the kitchen. Note the blue bead-board ceiling, the traditional choice for porches.

A basement or attached garage may feel disconnected from the rest of the house. You can remove the wall that conceals the basement stairs and replace it with a railing to make this gateway to the level below more open and inviting. A garage may involve a more difficult transition because its former use will be tricky to disguise. Nevertheless, with a larger opening and broad steps, a garage can become an inviting den, home theater, or sunken family room.

You can also enlarge interior space by building a cantilevered closet into the garage. It's not necessary to infringe on the parking area if you make sure the bottom of the closet sits high enough that a car can pull in beneath.

Attics typically can be integrated more easily than garages and basements because they sit directly above the house and may be accessed from any of several locations. When designing an attic remodel, consider adding more than just a stairway. By opening a portion of the ceiling below to create a lightwell, you can flood the center of the home with daylight, revitalizing an old, tired hallway or living room and creating a dramatic interior vista.

A stoop or front porch can be turned into an entrance hall with windows, an elegant door, and a tiled floor. Even if your house sits right on the front yard setback, your municipality may allow you to enclose the porch or stoop—a little-known exception in most zoning codes. Although it may seem that all you gain by enclosing the porch is a foyer, you are actually expanding the space within. By moving the entrance into what was once your old stoop or porch, you can reincorporate the former entry into the living area of your house.

While the transitional public-to-private appeal of a front porch will typically be diminished by enclosing it, back porches lend

Turning a potential liability into an asset, a Colorado Springs, Colo., couple accented the change in floor elevations between their house and garage conversion with a flight of custom-fabricated steps.

From Coach House to Couch Den

If you aren't making full use of a two-car garage, you can remove the double overhead door, replace it with a single-stall door, and reclaim half the garage for a den, office, or exercise room. To integrate this new room with the rest of the house, join the two with a generous opening of at least 6 ft.

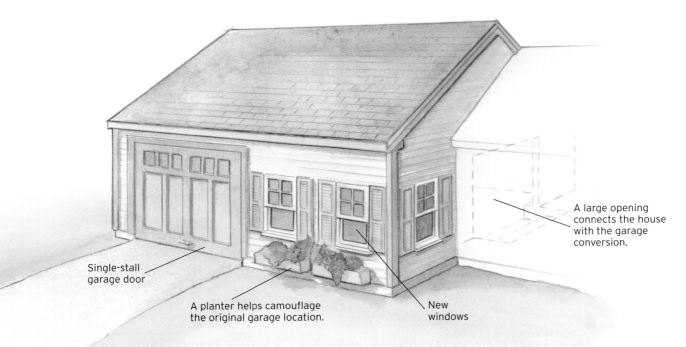

A large opening connects the house with the garage conversion.

Single-stall garage door

A planter helps camouflage the original garage location.

New windows

The low walls that separate this master bathroom from the bedroom save money in framing and also add architectural interest. Inside the bathroom, the toilet is set apart with full walls for privacy.

Columns recycled from another area of the house give the entry an elegant, traditional look at no added cost.

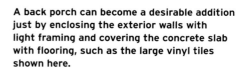
A back porch can become a desirable addition just by enclosing the exterior walls with light framing and covering the concrete slab with flooring, such as the large vinyl tiles shown here.

With the addition of a front porch, the old stoop can be brought indoors to provide a more distinctive foyer. In most cases, adding a porch won't run afoul of local set-back limitations.

Use large mirrors to double the apparent size of a small, cramped room. One approach is to remove the existing bypass or bifold doors and replace them with a mirrored version.

themselves to integration with the spaces inside. A new room at the back of the house allows you to enjoy the yard without enduring the weather. The key is creating an inviting transition that makes you want to enter this new room, not by emphasizing the door, but by widening the opening to create views to the landscape beyond.

Enlarging a room does not always mean adding floor space. You can increase the room's volume by bumping up the ceiling a few feet into the attic, cutting in a skylight, or installing a transom window. You can even reclaim a few feet of crawl space by dropping the floor in a section of your house to set apart an area for special activities.

Whenever possible, use optical illusions to expand the sense of space in a small room:
■ Paint the walls a color that draws your attention to the perimeter of the room instead of the center of the room.
■ Install a window near a corner to provide a long, diagonal sight line across the room.
■ In a small bath or hallway, install a skylight or reclaim some attic space to create a vaulted ceiling.
■ Install large pieces of art, which work like windows to draw your eye into vistas that seem to lie beyond the four walls.

Cantilevering

You can add a small closet or bay window without bothering with a foundation by cantilevering floor joists up to 2 ft. If you simply extend the roofline just over the addition, you'll also save money on roof framing.

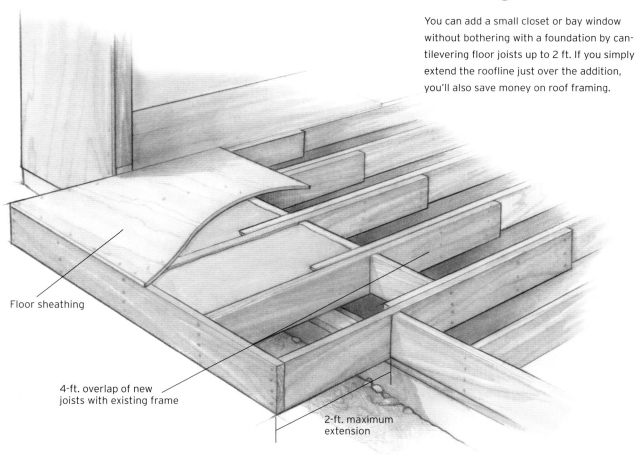

Floor sheathing

4-ft. overlap of new joists with existing frame

2-ft. maximum extension

■ Install a large mirror or mirrored wardrobe door to reflect light and to visually double the size of the room.

Adding On

Additions should remain your last choice from a cost perspective, but there are ways of adding on without compromising affordability. It may be possible to build a cantilever of up to 2 ft. without the expense of excavation and foundation work. Floor framing can usually extend that distance beyond the home's exterior if the new joists run at least 4 ft. within the existing structure. If you're able to limit the addition to the area covered by

the overhang of the roof, you can also avoid the cost of framing and shingling a separate roof for it. Or, if you want to provide more shelter, think about extending the pitch of the existing roofline to do the job rather than constructing an intersecting gable.

Another relatively inexpensive addition is to add one or more dormers. Dormers increase the headroom in the attic, thus increasing its usable space. They also bring in light and improve ventilation. A skylight is a simpler proposition, although it only modestly increases headroom.

The rooms of your house can be made to seem larger if you fashion an inviting tran-

This computer station at the end of a hall reclaims circulation space for a useful purpose, giving the kids a place to surf the Internet in plain view of the parents.

When remodeling, borrow freely from attractive homes you've seen either firsthand or in photographs. A talented homeowner glimpsed this impressive fireplace in a magazine and reproduced it on a smaller scale, achieving the same striking effect.

A new deck, patio, porch, or even simple three-season room costs considerably less than adding interior living space, with the related costs of insulation, heating and air-conditioning, and weathersealing.

PRO TIP

NOTHING TRANSFORMS A ROOM LIKE PAINT. From a rolled-on coat of flat background color to the edgy vanguard of faux finishing, paint is a low-cost way to revitalize a room and invite people to use it.

IF YOU DON'T HAVE A DESIGNER'S EYE, work within the color schemes offered by a particular brand of paint to achieve subtle, harmonious variety from room to room.

sition between indoors and out. This creates the desire to go a few steps farther—which, in effect, adds acreage to your residence. One of the best and least expensive ways of accomplishing this is to install an attractive combination of French or sliding patio doors and a picture window, with an easily accessible deck or patio beyond. Most houses already have a back door, of course, but it often serves merely as an exit rather than a welcoming passageway to the outdoors. So, try to visualize every door as an entry rather than an exit, as a beginning rather than an ending.

Design Development: Going with Your Best Strategy

Once your ideas have taken shape, *design development* is the stage at which you refine them into working drawings. If you took high school drafting or have an affinity for drawing, you should be able to come up with the drawings for a relatively simple project. Otherwise, you may want to hire a drafting service to create a formal set of floor plans. If you will be working with an architectural or design-build firm, they will take care of developing the drawings.

Whatever the case, you should remain closely involved with the process, because it's in the details that unexpected costs start creeping in. Always ask for frequent *progress prints* and study them carefully, looking for opportunities to tweak the plans to your satisfaction. Don't feel discouraged when problems creep up: The resourceful thinking that goes into solving design dilemmas often yields a solution more satisfying than the

original idea. An advantage of hiring a professional drafting or architectural service at this stage is that it may spot these problems early and suggest alternatives.

IDENTIFYING WHAT WORKS

When you find a photo of a room you like, note how the scale, color, textures, and furnishings work together. Perhaps you are struck by the crown molding, detailed window casing, or paneled ceiling. Maybe a thoughtful color palette brings about harmony. Or it could be that you are drawn to the textures established by the soft drapes, throw rug, and upholstery, which are in dramatic contrast to the hardwood floors and a stone wall.

It can be difficult to identify the elements that make the strongest impression. One way is to reduce the photograph to its essentials. Place a sheet of tracing paper over the

HUNTING FOR INSPIRATION

Gather ideas for your remodel by touring homes, new and old. Fully decorated houses may be on display at new subdivisions, and twice each year most chapters of the National Association of Home Builders have a weeklong Parade of Homes that highlights the best work of local builders. Neighborhood remodeling associations also offer home tours you can canvass for ideas; since homeowners host the tours, you may be able to ask questions about the details that appeal to you as well as get referrals for good contractors.

The copper band wrapping the front of this house looks like an expensive accent, but in fact it is a $500 galvanized-metal band finished with copper paint and "weathered" with verdigris antiquing.

photo and trace the major lines, horizontal and vertical, that define the room. Leave out all accessories and furniture as well as millwork like raised panels on doors, baseboards, window mullions, chair rails, and coffered ceilings. Indicate the windows as rectangles and squares, leaving out the drapes. Sketch cabinets as boxes without pulls, valances, or crowns. In other words, render the room without detail.

Next, compare this stripped-down drawing to the photo. You might be surprised that the drawing has nearly the same appeal. Another unexpected result may be that this room, without its trimmings, looks more than a little like a "before" picture of your existing house, which is a clue that you don't need remodeling, just interior decorating.

Now look back and forth between the photograph and the tracing until you determine the key to reproducing the desired effect. Let's say you think it's the color. Lay another

Instead of spending tens of thousands on hardwood bookshelves, the owner of this house chose a design that combined inexpensive drywall with cherry shelving at a fraction of the cost of solid wood bookcases.

THE SPARING USE OF A FEW EXPENSIVE PRODUCTS can create an aura that upgrades an entire room. In this case, expensive Italian tiles top the firebox, with cheap garden slate used to tile the hearth and wall.

PRO TIP

WITH SO MANY CHOICES ON THE MARKET TODAY, it pays to narrow your selection criteria. Before settling on specifics such as wall colors and tile patterns, chose product lines within your price range and then select from this affordable palette.

To ensure affordability and good aesthetics, I have a talented interior designer create interior palettes using my choice of inexpensive finishes. In the same way, you can shop for product lines and styles you can afford to fall in love with, then ask a fee-based designer to help you refine the selection.

piece of tracing paper over your rendering and copy it, so that you preserve the original drawing and can use it over again. Lay this second sketch over the photograph. Use colored pencils to duplicate the colors and shading in the room. Look at this version of the drawing and see if it comes close to the impression created by the photo. If it doesn't quite hit the mark, add the moldings and other details that complete the room's color scheme.

By adding and subtracting one detail at a time, you begin to develop a sense of the relative importance of scale, color, and texture. Sometimes a plain molding will convey the same sense of scale as an elaborate one, and at significant savings. Perhaps you leave out the molding entirely and just use paint on the lower third of the wall to suggest

wainscoting. The challenge is to distill the design to its essence so that you can omit expensive embellishments that aren't necessary for a high-end result.

Economizing does not always preclude using top-of-the-line products and luxurious materials. Often, it just means setting a moderate number of these items against an understated backdrop. For example, combine cherry cabinets with painted ones, or add a tile backsplash to a laminate counter. Look for opportunities to use expensive materials in a limited way and still achieve an effect. In a guest bathroom, just a small amount of glass tile reflected in the mirror, combined with a wallpaper wainscoting, makes a plain privy look pricey.

With a household paint line like Ralph Lauren® offering color palettes for everything

A home in a historic neighborhood may have architectural and environmental advantages that would be difficult or impossible to reproduce affordably. In this house, the corbels along the soffits, the Victorian detailing around the windows, and the whimsical corner balcony would add at least 10 percent to the cost of new construction.

from warm, traditional styles to jazzy "Island Brights," you can bring home elements of the best interior design without the cost. Use schemes like these to help you realize your favorite rooms, whether they are in your collection of magazine clippings or in houses that you've visited.

Getting Help with a Design

When I need professional assistance, I consult a trusted interior designer for her advice, not for her high-end merchandise. I choose a selection of affordable finishes, from paint swatches to plastic laminates, and she coordinates them. You can save a lot of money by paying an hourly rate for professional services and bypassing the designer's expensive line of furniture, carpets, and tiles. Start by spending a few hours window-shopping. Although you will not be buying anything at this stage, bring your floor plans to various stores and ask for price estimates specific to your project. Then pick the most affordable brands and styles of flooring, paint, cabinets, counters, and light fixtures appropriate for your project.

Remember that a remodeling project involves many layers of work, so don't become attached to a $9,000 cabinet selection when you have a $10,000 total budget. This is an obvious example, but you'll be surprised how much the trimmings cost, including accessories and final changes. Discipline yourself to select the least expensive brands and styles that provide the function and appearance you require. Once you have a range of choices in every category that fits your finances, bring the list to your designer along

OLD HOUSE HANDBOOKS

One way to get to know how your house once looked is to browse through out-of-print handbooks for carpenters, available at the library or through the Internet. Choose a source that was published around the time your house was built. Beyond including information on framing and foundations, these books may picture period architectural details, helping you ensure the authenticity of your remodeling.

HISTORIC OPPORTUNITIES

Rehabilitation building codes may allow you to obtain non-standard-use designations for a property in exchange for preserving its historic architecture. For example, you might restore a historic house in a residential neighborhood and then be able to run a bed-and-breakfast or serve high tea as a business, despite the residential zoning. My construction company office is a historical property zoned for residential use. In exchange for preserving the building, we are able to occupy half of the property as a showroom and office suite, while the other half is an elegant apartment.

IF YOU HAVE A GREEN BUILDING MATERIALS SUPPLIER IN YOUR AREA, check out the range of attractive ecological products now available. These include linoleum, cork, slate, recycled glass tile, bamboo, clay plaster, and paper-based fiber composites. Beyond their environmental advantages, these surfaces bring unusual textures and colors into the home.

Behind a plaster wall, the owner of this Victorian home found an abandoned fireplace. Although the firebox was inoperable, he refinished the highly detailed mantel in a nod to bygone days when the house was warmed by three fireplaces.

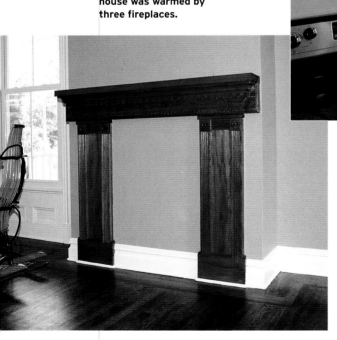

This brick chimney, originally covered up by a thick layer of boring plaster, now adds character to the kitchen remodel.

Remodeling can be something of a treasure hunt. When we pulled up this faded linoleum, we discovered oak flooring.

with the maximum price you'd be willing to pay. If you don't have a specific product in mind, provide a generic description (such as plastic laminate flooring) or a cost allowance (such as $15 a square yard).

Historical Rehab

The remodeling of an older home brings with it challenges and opportunities. You likely will work with details, materials, and workmanship that would be difficult to reproduce at any cost. The home may fit the surrounding landscape and seem as if it belongs where it is. Also, chances are it was built to suit the climate, even if its insulation and air-conditioning systems need updating.

Best of all, older homes have what I think of as buried treasure. You might discover quartersawn oak flooring under old carpeting or an original fireplace under a patch of plaster. You could choose to expose a brick chimney stack to show off its attractive masonry. A leaded-glass window in the stairway could become an accent if you refinish the frame. Survey your home for these hidden gems, then try to incorporate them into your plan.

Not every material you find in an older house needs to remain in place. You might remove moldings and other handsome details for reuse in this remodel or in a future project. An old marble countertop could become the focal point of the kitchen by installing it on an island. Salvaging building materials may be labor intensive, but it's less expensive than buying new moldings or fixtures.

With today's eclectic styles, you can freely mix and match materials, honoring historical elements without becoming a slave to authenticity. Experiment with a harmonious mix of materials, textures, and colors, contrasting soft and hard surfaces such as natural wood and steel, or combining painted millwork with natural wood finishes. Historical details, such as mosaic floors or a claw-foot tub, can be used in combination with modern fixtures, blending the best of old and new.

MODERN DECOR PALES BY COMPARISON

As you peel away layers of paint and wallpaper like an archaeologist on a dig, you may discover that people were once unafraid to brighten their homes with color. Kitchens boasted bright yellow walls, porch ceilings were coated sky blue, and bathrooms had frilly wallpaper. To find adventurous colors that might make your home a standout, refer to period collections of swatches offered by major paint manufacturers.

This home's banister system did not meet current codes, but we were able to save the distinctive 1800s newel post when installing a banister and balustrade to satisfy the building inspector.

Photo by Roe A. Osborn

CONSTRUCTION DRAWINGS: GETTING TO THE NITTY-GRITTY

In the last phase of drawing up plans, *construction drawings* are made to guide you or your contractor through the construction process. They include information like the size of joists, beams, and headers; smoke detector locations; plug and switch layouts; and other technical specifications needed to clearly communicate your intent and to comply with code requirements.

The local building department will need to see construction drawings before issuing permits. In a simple remodel, these drawings might fit on one page, featuring a floor plan of the alterations drawn to scale. A complex project could require a multipage set of documents with elevations (views of the home's exterior), sections (vertical views of the home's interior), and construction details.

Comply with the Code

Once you have a basic plan for remodeling, but before you start work, visit the building inspector. Building inspectors are more than a legal necessity. They provide an extra pair of eyes for quality control and health and safety measures. Many inspectors are former contractors with years of on-the-job experience—a potential bonus for do-it-yourselfers if this official is willing to serve as an integral part of the construction team.

If you plan on getting involved with the details of your remodel, you'll need to be familiar with the building code. All of the construction methods discussed in this book can be found in the *International Residential Code®* (IRC), now in force across most of the United States. It is the most progressive code to date, including many alternative building techniques that can help you remodel more affordably, such as advanced framing techniques with 24-in. on center stud

When adding new features, you don't have to be a slave to the existing style. Kitchen designer Carolyn Murray confidently combined traditional painted cabinets with decidedly 21st-century oak and the latest appliances.

Same Size, Bigger Experience

Starting with a puny and unpleasant bathroom, the designers at SawHorse Construction created a pleasing spa by opening up the layout with French doors and stretching a whimsical vanity right into the shower. The large diagonal floor tiles incorporate the passage area between doors with the room itself, making the space feel larger even though the overall dimensions didn't change.

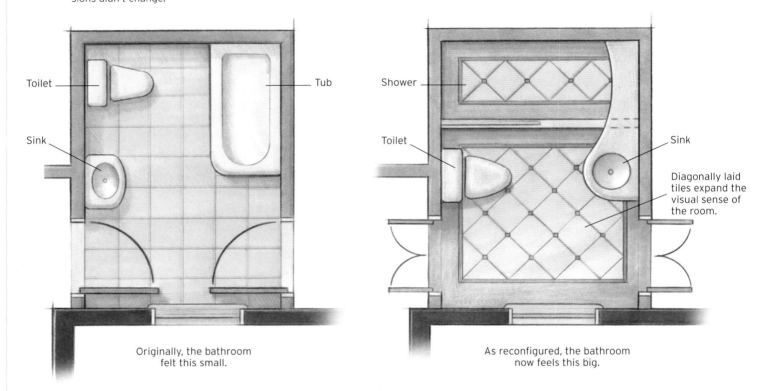

Toilet — Tub

Sink

Originally, the bathroom felt this small.

Shower — Sink

Toilet

Diagonally laid tiles expand the visual sense of the room.

As reconfigured, the bathroom now feels this big.

spacing and wood foundations. You'll find a long list of rules and guidelines that specify how to safely and soundly construct and remodel. In areas prone to earthquakes and hurricanes, local building codes reflect these dangers and enforce stricter guidelines for structural systems.

By meeting with a building official, you'll learn which documents and drawings your municipality requires before issuing a building permit. If your project includes moving walls, you will need at least a floor plan showing room sizes and uses as well as an indication of existing walls and those you

plan to remove or add. A plan reviewer will study your drawings and make comments, and he or she might also point out the need for smoke detectors in a hallway or ask about the window sizes in a bedroom.

Erasing and redrawing lines on paper is always cheaper than tearing out and rebuilding, so it pays to learn these requirements during the planning phase rather than during construction. Once you know your plans meet code standards and you have a building permit to prove it, you are ready to roll up your sleeves and get to work.

Ordinary Made Extraordinary

An architect's house may work double duty as a home and a personal display of his or her design creativity. Cash-strapped architect Jim Zack, of Zack/de Vito Architecture in San Francisco, had to be doubly ingenious when remodeling his 1912 Edwardian flat because it was necessary to pinch pennies. Zack's concept was to knit modern elements into a restored historical shell, saving money by "using ordinary materials in unexpected ways," as he explains.

Fortunately, the original house had "good bones," meaning that it possessed a sound structure and a layout that lent itself to easy remodeling. Instead of the usual row-house floor plan with a long corridor and successive rooms, this flat featured rooms set around a square central hall. Zack used the principle of subtraction to make the home feel more spacious by removing walls and combining rooms. And he took advantage of the unfinished attic's 12-ft. ceilings by turning it into a grand master-bedroom suite.

Photo by Jim Zack

To save money, Jim Zack built his own cabinets, laminated a bowed sheet of plywood with stainless-steel sheet metal over a $25 range hood, poured his own concrete countertops, and refinished the existing floors.

Photo by Jim Zack

Although working with steel may seem intimidating, Zack says that cutting, welding, and building with metal is no more difficult than carpentry. With tools available at the local home center, Zack built this stairway and lined his doorways with steel jambs for a modern, high-end look that cost little more than standard construction.

3

Getting Dirty

BEFORE YOU CAN ENJOY YOUR DREAM KITCHEN, master suite, or comfy den, you have to roll up your sleeves and make some dust. For the avid remodeler, this is the fun part. For others, it's just a rough road toward a desirable end. Either way, in order to have money left over for attractive cabinets, paints, and flooring materials, you need to budget the bones of your project in the rough stages of construction.

But when it comes to demolition, foundations, and framing, it can appear that there's only one choice: to do it the way it's always been done. In fact, the rough stages of remodeling offer you many new materials and methods that can improve an older home's economy, durability, and energy efficiency.

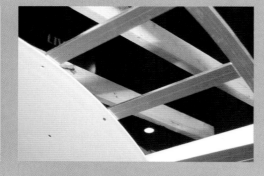

By watching the budget on what goes inside walls and under floors, you'll be able to spend more on the aspects of the remodeling that show.

HOUSEHOLD HAZARDS

Unfortunately, old houses can be full of unpleasant surprises that come to light as you work. Here's a review of common problems and pitfalls, with suggestions on how to approach them.

Knob-and-Tube Wiring

In the early 1900s, electricians strung double strands of insulated wire along ceramic knobs and through ceramic tubes in the framing. This wiring cannot carry today's heavy demands. What's more, dried-out wires can fray and burn when overheated. If such a system is still in place when it comes time to remodel, replace the new areas with sheathed cable and modern circuit breakers.

Undersize Amps

Your house may not provide enough electricity. A telltale sign is if the lights dim when you run the vacuum cleaner. An insufficient system itself does not necessarily pose a hazard. But it usually will have too few outlets, meaning there will be too many extension cords snaking through the home, which can pose a fire hazard. If you're going

to remodel, update the electrical panel and add circuits to all the heavy-use areas such as kitchen, garage, and laundry. Update bathroom, kitchen, garage, and exterior outlets to ground-fault circuit-interrupter (GFCI) circuits or outlets.

Steel Water Pipes

Until about 1940, most plumbing was made of steel pipe. Steel pipe rusts and eventually leaks; also, it corrodes to shrink the interior diameter to a trickle. Couplings tend to rust and fail, too. If steel pipes serve the area you will remodel, replace them with a modern alternative such as PEX, CPVC, or copper. PEX plastic pipe has the advantage of flexibility, allowing you to snake it through existing framing and other remodeling obstacles.

Lead-Based Paint

Lead was as an ingredient in house paint up until 1978, and it's thought that 75 percent of all homes built before that date contain some lead paint. Lead poses a serious health hazard, and it is made airborne by scraping and sanding during remodeling. Young children may swallow paint chips and children and adults

Knob-and-tube wiring is inherently unsafe and should be replaced as part of any remodeling project.

Photo by Ellen Kunz

can inhale lead dust. If you are in doubt about whether paint contains lead, use test strips sold at paint stores and home centers. Or contact the state health department for information on having a test done for you.

According to the Consumer Product Safety Commission, you should only attempt removing lead-based paint in a limited area, using wet scraping, wet sanding, or a liquid paint stripper to avoid dust. Restrict yourself to paint that is chipping or bubbling, rather than working on surfaces that are in reasonably good condition. Or you can replace chipped trim and avoid a mess altogether. Safer still, hire a certified lead abatement contractor.

Wear disposable coveralls, waterproof gloves, and a HEPA (high-efficiency particulate air) respirator rather than a common dust mask. When scraping or sanding, mist the area with water to hold down dust, catch the residue, and place it in a garbage bag. When you are done, wash the area with a solution of 1 tablespoon of trisodium phosphate (TSP) in a gallon of water. Rinse with clear water and allow the area to dry before painting. Clean the room thoroughly with a damp cloth or mop; a vacuum cleaner will only spread lead dust throughout your house unless it is equipped with an industrial-grade HEPA filter.

Asbestos Alert

In older homes, you are most likely to encounter asbestos in duct and water pipe insulation, vermiculite attic insulation, acoustical ceiling tile, and floor and ceiling tiles. To know what you may be up against, hire a

BEFORE

Demo is not just about tearing out walls and floors. You can also remove paint to renew the appearance, function, and durability of old surfaces. Christopher and Ellen Kunz of Neenah, Wis., used a stripper to take off the flooring mastic and varnish from an old Douglas fir subfloor. This hidden treasure was treated to sanding and a clear coat of polyurethane.

TIPS FOR PROPER PREP

At the end of a remodeling project, much time may be spent patching dings and cleaning up messes that could have been avoided. Take a few precautions before getting started, and you'll be more efficient overall.

- Protect floors with building paper and canvas drop cloths for light demolition; add a layer of bargain-priced damaged sheathing for heavy work.
- Protect adjacent walls by putting up building paper with painter's tape. Cover windows with a sheet of particleboard, secured with screws or double-headed nails.
- Isolate the work area from the rest of the home with sheets of 6-mil plastic, sealing edges with painter's tape. Even if you can close off a room by shutting a door, dust will find its way though the cracks, so cover the doorway by taping up a sheet of plastic.
- Shut off the utilities to the room—both power and water. It is all too easy to inadvertently cut or drill into a wire or pipe.

technician to conduct an asbestos survey. If you suspect asbestos in a limited area, place a sample in a sandwich bag and take it to a testing lab. Asbestos removal specialists can effectively rid a home of this menace, and they follow legally prescribed disposal methods.

The Radioactive Basement

In some parts of the country, naturally occurring radon gas enters homes through the foundation. Radon is radioactive and poses a significant cancer risk at higher levels. You can buy a radon detection kit to test your home for radon. The kit's manufacturer will then test the sample and report back to you. If your house has radon levels above maximum levels set by the Environmental Protection Agency (EPA), consider hiring a contractor to install a sealing and ventilation system.

INSPIRED DECONSTRUCTION

Remodeling usually begins not with construction, but with removing parts of the old structure to make room for improvements. It's called *demolition*, although that sounds like something you should never try at home. A better term, borrowed from the world of fine art, is *deconstruction*. Properly done, deconstruction is the delicate process of selective subtraction in order to make room for your new floor plan. Consider it as peeling away layers of trim and cladding to reveal the fundamental nature of your house.

The secret to cost-effective deconstruction lies in not removing too much. Instead, select the elements you want to remove and carefully protect the rest. That's why the first step in deconstruction should look a lot like

TOOLS OF THE DEMOLITION TRADE

You'll need more than a hammer and broom to do the job. Here is a list of tools and supplies that will come in handy when you remodel.

- Nail puller
- Claw hammer
- 1-lb. sledgehammer
- Crowbar
- Steel chisel
- Utility knife
- Reciprocating saw with metal and wood blades
- Screwdriver or screw gun
- Dustpan and brush
- Heavy-duty vacuum

The smaller tools are useful for removing trim that you plan on reusing. Use a steel chisel, utility knife, and drywall saw to take out sections of drywall. The crowbar, sledgehammer, and reciprocating saw will make quick work of clearing away framing. And the need for a powerful shop vacuum will soon make itself apparent.

DRESS FOR DEMO SUCCESS

The essential couture includes a fitted respirator for fine and potentially harmful dust particles, safety glasses (or side guards for your prescription lenses), a pair of flexible work gloves, earplugs when using power tools, and a hard hat when demolishing a ceiling.

MANY CITIES HAVE A RECYCLING CENTER FOR CONSTRUCTION and demolition debris. And you are likely to generate a lot of it: A typical kitchen or bathroom remodel can create as much debris as a household puts out for curbside recycling in four years.

PRO TIP

you're painting. You mask floors, tape off adjacent surfaces, lay drop cloths, and erect dust barriers. Some of the mightiest tools of demolition include crowbars, hatchets, and sledgehammers, but in deconstruction you'll more likely need a drywall knife, reciprocating and circular saws, a screw gun, a cat's paw, a hammer, and a putty knife.

Always try to deconstruct in the reverse order of construction. Start with fixtures, counters, and trim. Move on to cabinets and doors. The last stage is removing walls and floors. Even when reconfiguring the floor plan, some delicacy is called for. Injuries that occur during demolition are usually the result of swinging a sledgehammer or violently prying something loose.

To remove and save the trim, gently pry it loose with a small painter's prybar, sliding a putty knife under the bar so that you don't damage the wall. Remove nails from the trim by pulling them through from behind to avoid harming the visible surface.

To remove drywall (known also as gypsum board or Sheetrock®), score the edges of the wall with a drywall knife and then cut out and pull off manageable-size rectangles. Begin removing studs from the bottom by cutting the nails with a reciprocating saw. Generally, try to *cut and remove* rather than *tear off*. The process should never feel brutal.

To Gut or Not to Gut

In building-trade terms, *gutting* a house

In remodeling jargon, gutting means removing the wall finish to expose the framing. This step makes it easier to run new wires and pipes, but it also makes a mess and adds substantially to the cost of reconstruction. Remove wall coverings only where necessary— even if the electrician or plumber grumbles about the inconvenience.

Cutting Plaster Cleanly

To remove a section of lath-and-plaster wall neatly, begin by shutting off the power to the room, and take care to avoid cutting any wiring or plumbing. Attach 1x4s to the studs with screws, then cut along a straight-edge with a reciprocating saw. For the horizontal edges, make sure to cut between parallel strips of lath.

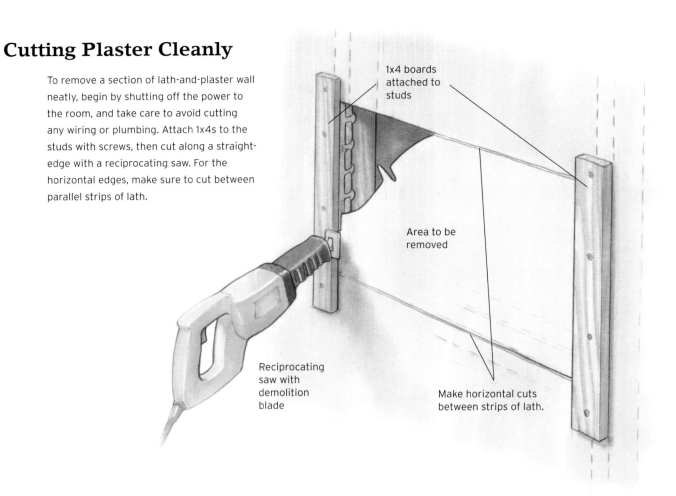

1x4 boards attached to studs

Area to be removed

Reciprocating saw with demolition blade

Make horizontal cuts between strips of lath.

In this cross section, you can see how plaster locks into the spaces between strips of wood lath. Successive coats are built up for a smooth finish, in spite of the rough wood used for framing.

means removing the wall and ceiling coverings and taking the rooms back to the bare studs. It's tempting to gut a room before remodeling because it seems so much easier to start from scratch. Electricians can rope wire, plumbers can run pipe, and you can insulate and cover the walls with new drywall to a perfect finish. But, gutting is usually a mistake and often occurs by accident. You don't need to strip the walls to insulate or to run wires. You can install new drainpipes and ducts by removing a segment of wall or ceiling rather than the whole thing.

At times, however, it pays to strip a wall when remodeling an area, such as a kitchen, that will require extensive plumbing and electrical work. This is especially true if your walls are plaster. Unlike drywall, plaster over *lath*—rough, yardstick-like strips of wood—tends to act like a fabric. Tugging on one section causes the entire fabric to unravel. Many total gut jobs begin unintentionally when an enthusiastic amateur tries to work on a small section of wall and ends up removing all the plaster in the room.

Hassling with Plaster and Lath

To work effectively with plaster and lath, it's good to understand how these walls were made. Builders attached lath across studs in rows about $\frac{3}{8}$ in. apart. Plasterers covered the lath with a coarse layer of wet plaster called the *scratch coat*. The plaster squeezed through gaps in the lath, locking this layer into the lath. The plasterers then raked the surface to provide a textured surface to grip the next layer. Days later, when the first coat had dried, the *brown coat* went on, making the walls roughly flat. Finally, a *skim coat* of pure white plaster produced the finished surface.

Cut Short of the Ceiling

Whenever possible, stop the removal short of a corner, cutting a parallel line about 6 in. away with a circular saw and masonry blade.

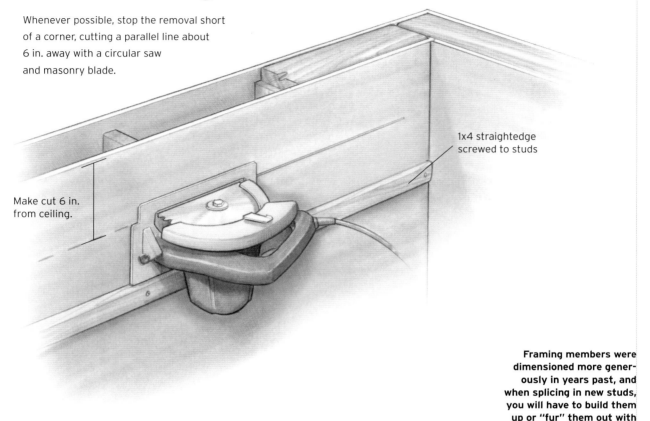

Make cut 6 in. from ceiling.

1x4 straightedge screwed to studs

Framing members were dimensioned more generously in years past, and when splicing in new studs, you will have to build them up or "fur" them out with strips of lath to match the beefier lumber.

Fast-forward 75 years, and this wood lath may have dried out, loosening its grip on the plaster. This shows up as bulges and breaks in walls and especially ceilings of old homes. You'll make matters worse if you strike damaged plaster with a hammer. And if you try to cut a section with a reciprocating saw, the vibration may shake the rest loose. To avoid a mess, find the studs on either side of the damaged or unwanted area and run a 1x4 between them, attaching it with screws so that it tightly holds the plaster in place. You'll then be able to make vertical cuts in the plaster with a reciprocating saw without the wood lath vibrating and coming loose. Use a circular saw with a masonry blade to make horizontal cuts.

If you try to pull off plaster high up on a wall, you're likely to remove plaster from the ceiling as well. As a precaution, use a circular

saw to score a 1-in.-deep cut along the wall about 6 in. below the ceiling.

Cover the area you've removed with ⅝-in.-thick drywall and tape the plaster-to-drywall seam. If the plaster is too thick for a smooth transition, add a layer of ⅜-in. drywall over a ½-in. sheet, and you should have a close-enough match to effectively feather the seam with drywall compound.

After stripping off plaster and lath, you may find that the framing is rough and twisted. You can replace the worst offenders, then level out the rest with thin pieces of lath glued and nailed to the face of the stud. Follow with ⅝-in.-thick drywall, which tends to hide framing defects better than its ½-in. cousin. Or save yourself trouble by leaving the old plaster in place as a smooth base for a new layer of drywall. Apply the drywall with construction adhesive and 2½-in. drywall screws, covering any holes you've made for plumbing and wiring.

If you're only dealing with cracked plaster, try a specialty product such as extra-wide self-adhesive Super Crackstop®. This mesh tape is made of strong fiberglass yarns, and it requires only a thin coat of drywall compound for a smooth finish.

OTHER WALLS, OTHER METHODS

Besides plaster walls with wood lath, you might encounter other materials when remodeling. Button board was a predecessor to drywall, consisting of gypsum sheets with punctures (buttons) that plasterers could simply nail onto the framing and then cover with a topcoat as a one-step finish. To remove button board, cut it with a utility knife and pull. You may also find metal lath, which, if disturbed, can loosen surrounding plaster. You have to cut through metal lath before removing a section of wall. A reciprocating-saw blade tends to stick in the wire mesh, so use a circular saw with a blade intended to cut metal.

PLYWOOD BOX BEAMS

Box beams are site-built beams that typically consist of conventional wall-framing lumber (usually 2x4s or 2x6s) sandwiched between two plywood gussetts. They are the least expensive code-prescribed option for bearing spans 4 ft. to 8 ft. You can also build a box beam with only one plywood gussetts, but this will have considerably less strength.

TAKING AWAY WALLS

You know you're in the thick of remodeling when you start removing walls—the point of no return. Unlike construction, which can take days or months to complete, deconstruction delivers instant gratification: A wall goes away, and you have a new floor plan.

The procedure for removing a nonbearing wall is simple. Mask off the rooms on both sides of the wall. Protect floors, windows, and anything subject to damage, and shut off power to the rooms. Cut or score the perimeter of your demolition area to avoid taking down more than you planned, and begin by

Safely removing a bearing wall can entail shoring both sides of the ceiling, especially if joists lap above the condemned wall.

If your old walls have deteriorated and the remodeling process has damaged the surface substantially, consider placing a thin layer of drywall right over the existing surface. This may mean adding jamb extensions on windows and door frames or, alternatively, using round drywall corner bead for a no-casing look.

Temporary Walls

While making an opening in a bearing wall, such as for a window, you have to support the weight of the floor and roof above with shoring. The easiest way to accomplish this is by building a temporary wall out of 2x4s. Place the wall within 2 ft. of the area to be removed.

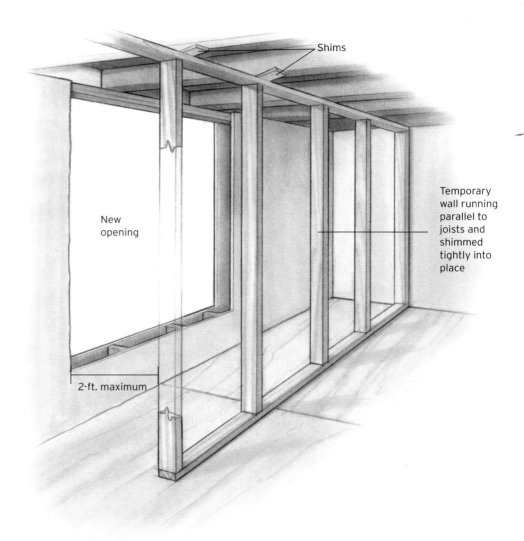

Shims

New opening

Temporary wall running parallel to joists and shimmed tightly into place

2-ft. maximum

removing the wall surface. Again, you deconstruct using the same sequence as construction, but in reverse. Once the studs are bare, check the wall for wires, ducts, and pipes.

Next, use a reciprocating saw with a metal-cutting or demolition blade to cut through the nails that attach the studs to the bottom plate. If necessary, tap the stud free by knocking out the lower end with a mallet, holding the stud with one hand so it won't come flying off. You generally will not need to cut the nails at the top because you can easily pull off the studs once the lower end is freed. Having removed the studs, you can now pull out any remaining nails and stockpile the studs for later.

To remove the top plates, use the reciprocating saw to cut these horizontal pieces into

4-ft. sections or smaller, then free them with a prybar. Protect the adjacent ceiling by placing a 1x4 under the prybar to distribute its pressure over a wider area. Any damage you do now will take time and money to fix.

Removing a Bearing Wall

Bearing walls carry floor and ceiling loads down to the foundation. Removing them is not that different from taking out other walls, but you do have to temporarily support the structure above while removing one structural element and replacing it with another. Otherwise sagging floors, cracked plaster, and unanticipated repairs may result.

The usual approach to removing an interior bearing wall requires one (or sometimes two) temporary *shoring walls* parallel with it

YOU NEED A PERMIT TO ALTER A BEARING WALL,
but you typically don't to alter a nonbearing partition.
Check with your local building department.

and no more than 2 ft. away. The weight is then transferred onto the shoring, which in turn spreads it safely over a broad area. When removing only a portion of a wall, such as to add a door or pass-through, I use a different strategy. I temporarily nail an appropriate-size header board onto the studs at the top of both sides of the wall, creating a structural sandwich that transfers the load from the area I intend to remove to the adjacent framing. The size of the headers depends on the width of the opening; two 2x6s suffice for a 3-ft.-wide door, while two 2x10s would generally carry a 6-ft. opening. Attach the boards with three double-headed 10-penny nails at each stud. Once a permanent header is over the new opening, remove the temporary boards.

For openings of up to 6 ft., consider building a plywood box header that acts as both temporary shoring and permanent support. Start by stripping the plaster or drywall off the wall where you will install the header. Then glue and nail a sheet of ½-in. plywood to one side of the wall, extending at least 6 in. beyond the opening width. This plywood gusset temporarily holds the opening as you complete the header construction. It can then serve as a permanent header.

Make sure to protect the floor under the temporary wall with a sheet of particleboard or a carpet remnant. Carpet also works well to protect ceilings when you install a temporary wall.

Removing a Ceiling

You may want to remove a section of ceiling to open the second floor to the first, which

can pose challenges even for a seasoned remodeler. The complexity of the job depends in part on the direction in which the joists run. It's easiest to make an opening parallel to the framing. And if the opening lies within 3 ft. of a bearing wall and does not exceed 4 ft. in width, you can usually remove the floor joists and frame the opening with a single 2x10 on each side, as shown in the drawing on p. 60. For openings perpendicular to the framing, temporary walls must support the floor loads. First remove an area around the desired opening wide enough to install double joists the full length of the room, then attach the existing framing members to these new joists with joist hangers. It's a big deal, so mull the cost and benefits before plunging in.

To bring light into an interior space, you may be able to strip away part of the ceiling and create a lightwell extending up to the roof.

Stair Openings

An opening parallel to the floor joists can be easy to frame, requiring only one header, no framing hardware (or hangers), and single trimmers. Whenever you can place an opening in line with the floor framing, you'll save money.

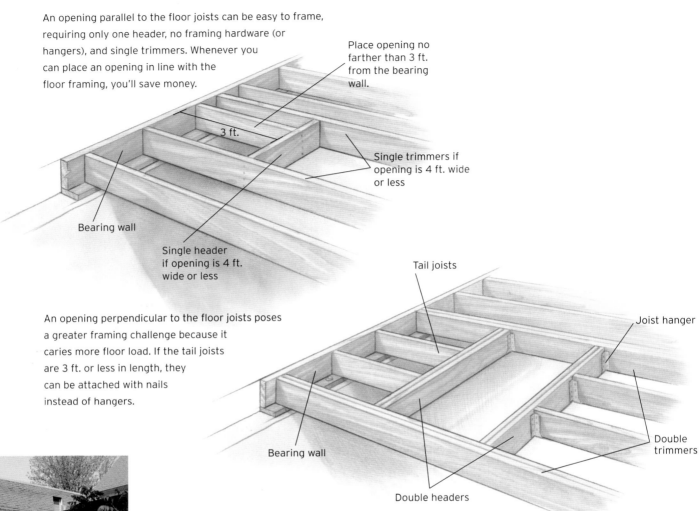

Place opening no farther than 3 ft. from the bearing wall.

3 ft.

Single trimmers if opening is 4 ft. wide or less

Bearing wall

Single header if opening is 4 ft. wide or less

An opening perpendicular to the floor joists poses a greater framing challenge because it caries more floor load. If the tail joists are 3 ft. or less in length, they can be attached with nails instead of hangers.

Tail joists

Joist hanger

Double trimmers

Bearing wall

Double headers

Major foundation repairs are disruptive and expensive, but unfortunately they're a necessary part of some remodeling jobs. You can save money by keeping your mind open to new foundation technologies that make restoration easier than in the past.

A BETTER FOUNDATION FROM THE GROUND UP

An advantage of remodeling is that typically you don't have to deal with the foundation. But there are exceptions. When you remove a bearing wall and install posts, you may need to support the concentrated load of these posts onto a new footing. And if you live in an older house, sagging floors may signal the need for a beefed-up foundation.

Several effective but inexpensive foundation and footing options exist, including shallow frost-protected footings, insulated concrete blocks, and permanent wood foundations. If you're concerned about the environment, you can add to the list a few low-impact alternatives to Portland cement, such as cementlike recycled waste products.

FRAMING FUNDAMENTALS

Optimum value engineered (OVE) framing or *advanced framing* was developed in the 1970s to help reduce the cost of production housing. Since then, this system has become the favorite of green builders because it uses less lumber and works with modern insulation techniques to maximize energy efficiency. Among its fundamentals are 24-in. on-center

Arrested Development

Hydrostatic soil pressure may cause a basement wall to bulge. If aesthetics are not important, resist the movement by placing steel I-beams against the bulge. Secure the beams by bolting them to a perpendicular joist or to 2-by blocking that is run between three or more parallel joists, as shown. Set the beams in footings at least 12 in. below the slab.

2-by blocking nailed to joists

Bolts

I-beam embedded in concrete footing

Bulge in foundation wall

(o.c.) framing and the use of appropriately sized headers and beams instead of wasteful overbuilding.

Where wall framing is not structural, place 2x4 studs at 24-in. centers to reduce lumber costs roughly by a third, without compromising strength. The system works especially well for exterior walls, where the added spacing provides room for more insulation. The energy savings are greater still if you use such details as two-stud corners, insulated headers, and ladder-blocked wall intersections.

If you work with a contractor, ask about advanced framing techniques. If he or she responds knowledgeably, then you

WATERPROOFING ALTERNATIVES

A damp basement is virtually useless, even for storage. Concrete and block, the most common basement materials, are inherently porous and benefit from waterproofing and proper drainage on the outside. To spare yourself the expense of all that digging, you can apply an interior waterproof coating such as Thoro Systems Thoroseal® and Bonsal® Sure Coat®. These products act as a second line of defense, but for a fail-safe solution, you must apply waterproofing on the exterior surface as well. You can hire a mud-jacking contractor to pump bentonite clay outside the exterior walls to waterproof them without any digging, potentially saving you thousands of dollars.

EVEN IN A BEARING WALL, MOST WINDOWS AND DOORS 3 ft. wide or less require no more than a single 2x10 for a header. If your house has a 2x10 rim joist, this will usually suffice, making it unnecessary to add a separate header over the opening.

Sparing Lumber

Building walls with 24-in. on-center framing makes good sense in terms of cost, performance, and kindness to the environment. You also can save by using ladder blocking instead of three-stud corners to support drywall at wall intersections. Or, skip the extra blocking and studs by leaving a gap into which the drywall is slid.

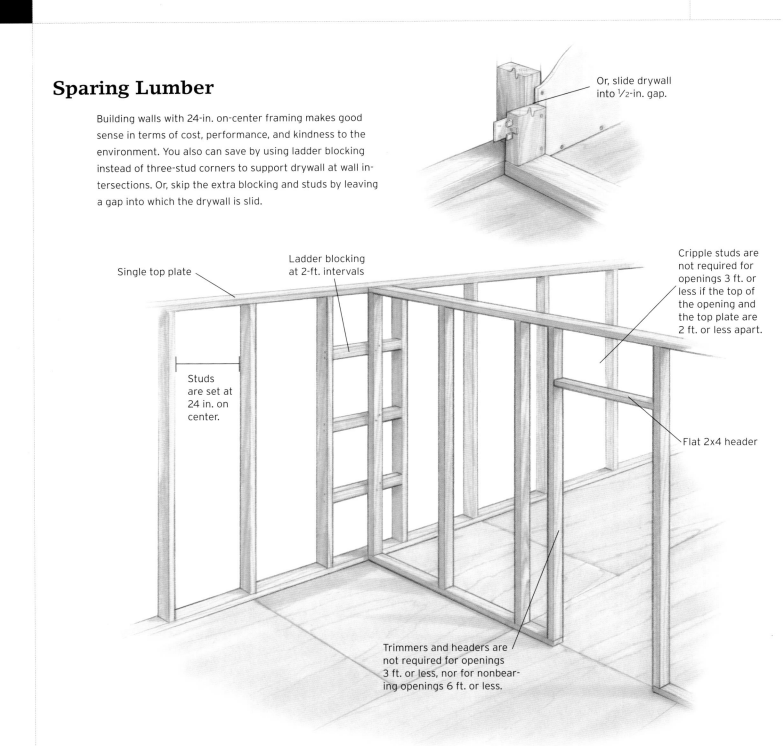

Or, slide drywall into 1/2-in. gap.

Single top plate

Ladder blocking at 2-ft. intervals

Cripple studs are not required for openings 3 ft. or less if the top of the opening and the top plate are 2 ft. or less apart.

Studs are set at 24 in. on center.

Flat 2x4 header

Trimmers and headers are not required for openings 3 ft. or less, nor for nonbearing openings 6 ft. or less.

have found someone who keeps abreast of progressive building techniques and will likely be sensitive to matters such as value engineering and energy efficiency.

Nonbearing Walls

I lay a 2x4 bottom plate across the floor where I want a new interior wall to go. For the top plate, I use ¾-in. material, which reduces the weight of an assembly that I'll eventually have to raise up. I mark stud centers at 24 in. at the same time on both top and bottom plates. I try to keep all openings on the 24-in. module by butting the left-hand side of any door or pass-through against a stud. The resulting layout makes it easier to attach wallboard later. This may mean shifting an opening a few inches from the planned location, but that's not usually a significant matter.

For an opening of 3 ft. or less, I use *king studs* running the full height of the wall, but no short *jack studs* between the header and

Photo courtesy of Hardy Frames, Inc.

When remodeling in an area vulnerable to hurricanes or earthquakes, you have to preserve the shear value of structural walls—their ability to resist the strong lateral forces imposed by wind and earth movement. If you will be installing a wide patio door or picture window, you can preserve the wall's lateral strength by using Hardy Frame® panels of light-gauge steel.

The abundant forests in North America, along with the traditional timber skills of English settlers, made wood the foremost building material in the United States and Canada.

Don't spend too much by overengineering interior walls. You can frame them economically by omitting the structural headers and double top plates.

Advanced Framing

The traditional method for building a partition wall wastes lumber and money. Advanced framing techniques are no less durable or structurally sound, and they allow you to put together a wall more quickly. Studs are set at 24-in. centers, there are no trimmers or headers at nonbearing openings, and only a single top plate is needed.

Traditional Framing

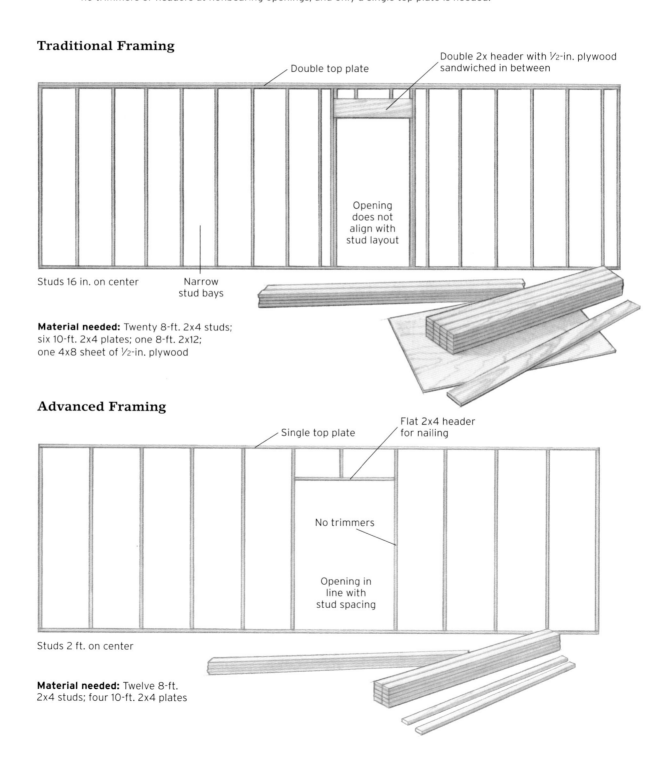

Double top plate

Double 2x header with ½-in. plywood sandwiched in between

Opening does not align with stud layout

Studs 16 in. on center

Narrow stud bays

Material needed: Twenty 8-ft. 2x4 studs; six 10-ft. 2x4 plates; one 8-ft. 2x12; one 4x8 sheet of ½-in. plywood

Advanced Framing

Single top plate

Flat 2x4 header for nailing

No trimmers

Opening in line with stud spacing

Studs 2 ft. on center

Material needed: Twelve 8-ft. 2x4 studs; four 10-ft. 2x4 plates

BECAUSE STEEL DOESN'T SUPPORT THE GROWTH OF MOLD,
metal studs are an ideal framing material for wet areas such
as bathrooms and kitchens. Although less familiar than wood,
steel studs are actually easier to work with.

bottom plate. My header is just a scrap 2x4 on edge. If the top plate and header span 2 ft. or less between them, I don't use *cripples* between the header and the plate. Attaching drywall on both sides of the wall provides the necessary strength.

To make sure that the new wall fits when lifted into place, I measure the smallest distance from floor to ceiling and make the wall 1½ in. shorter. I fill the gap with 2x4 scraps. Attaching the wall to the ceiling becomes a matter of toenailing the scraps to the ceiling joists. To prevent wall squeaks, I use construction adhesive and screws to attach the wall to the floor.

Metal Framing

Light-gauge steel framing is inexpensive, strong, and highly efficient, but few remodeling contractors and even fewer homeowners are familiar with it. In the highly competitive world of commercial contracting, however, builders use almost nothing else.

Steel studs are anchored within channels that are the equivalent of wooden bottom and top plates in conventional framing, but the similarities end there. You attach a channel to the ceiling with tech or drywall screws and then drop a plumb bob or aim a laser level to mark the position of the channel on the floor. This channel attaches to the floor with screws, meaning no future squeaks. Next, cut studs to length with tinsnips or a chopsaw fitted with a metal-cutting blade. Studs are set out on a roughly 24-in. layout and snap into place when given a twist. They can be adjusted as necessary as you put up the drywall so that you always have

You already may have all the equipment needed to frame with steel studs right in your toolbox, including a level, chalkline, tinsnips, plumb bob, cordless drill, and screw gun.

STRUCTURAL STEEL BEAMS

When replacing a stretch of bearing wall longer than 8 ft. with a structural beam, consider using a steel I-beam. A section of steel can easily carry the weight that would require a large, cumbersome wood beam. Always check the cost and weight of a steel beam before going with wood, especially for spans more than 16 ft.

ALL LIGHT-GAUGE STEEL FRAMING CONTAINS A MINIMUM OF 25 PERCENT RECYCLED CONTENT and is itself 100 percent recyclable—not that you'd be likely to have much left over as scrap after a remodeling. Steel job-site waste averages just 2 percent as opposed to 20 percent for wood.

Light-gauge steel framing is easy to work with and offers an excellent low-cost green building alternative for remodeling projects.

Cutting lightweight steel studs is a snap with tinsnips. After cutting the flanges, bend the stud back and cut through the web.

It's easy to attach steel studs to channels with hex screws.

Straps and Flanges

A sure cure for bouncy floors, this L-beam attached perpendicular to and under your floor joists at about 8 ft. on center will stiffen the floor assembly without requiring new joists, posts, or added footings.

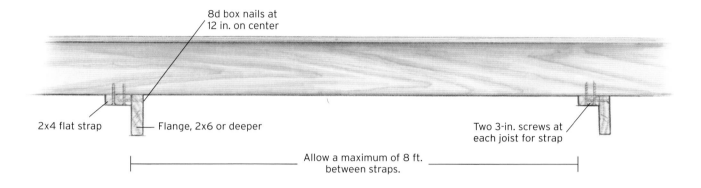

8d box nails at 12 in. on center

2x4 flat strap

Flange, 2x6 or deeper

Two 3-in. screws at each joist for strap

Allow a maximum of 8 ft. between straps.

a stud backing up the joints between sheets. You use tech screws only to fasten frames around openings.

Next, run wiring and plumbing through the prepunched holes in the studs. Finally, attach the drywall by driving screws into the studs and channels. The completed assembly is perfectly straight. The drywall serves as the primary stiffening element.

FIRMER FLOORS

Bouncy, squeaky floors are a common nuisance with older homes. You might also run into floor problems in a newer house built using overly flexible floor systems such as engineered long-span joists, improperly secured subfloors, and insufficient midspan blocking. All of these have inexpensive fixes. And if your remodel involves adding new floors, such as in an unfinished attic, you will want a modern floor system that won't bounce or squeak.

Banish the Bounce

Bounciness results from framing that is poorly supported or insufficiently stiff. Framing members often are compromised when improperly drilled or cut for wires and pipes, or when moisture and wood-eating insects have caused deterioration. Fixing these problems will be relatively easy if they affect the first floor and if the underside is accessible from the basement. On upper stories, a repair might entail removing portions of the ceiling or adding a dropped beam.

For the first floor, you could install a beam and add pier footings and posts, but you probably won't need to do more than add a *strongback*. Nail a continuous 2x4 strap under the joists, traversing them at about midspan. Next, nail a 2x6 to the 2x4 strap using 16-penny nails about every 16 in. The floor will become notably stiffer and quieter. You can also install this fix under a finished ceiling and then box out the strongback to make it look like a solid beam.

For a floor with uneven joists, consider a more creative albeit slightly more expensive solution. Hang doubled 2x6s from the joists at about midspan so that they are suspended from the joists using a double 2x12 joist hanger. Drive shims between the joist and the new double beam as needed so that the floor is supported evenly.

Old floor framing can present many challenges to the remodeler, from annoying squeaks to undersized and improperly supported joists. Fixing the underlying problems will go a long way toward making your house feel secure and comfortable.

Hanging a Beam

To stiffen a floor, you can hang a beam off the joists. This method works especially well with old floors framed with uneven lumber, using shims to bridge differences in joist depth.

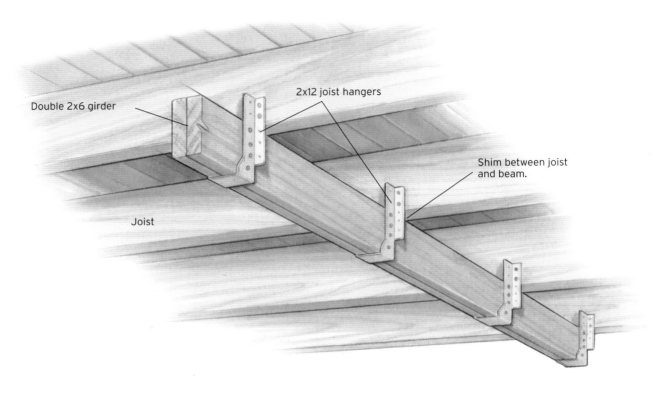

Double 2x6 girder

2x12 joist hangers

Shim between joist and beam.

Joist

If the joists are large enough for the span but still bouncy, inspect the connection between the joists and beams. For floor joists that are notched or simply nailed into a girder, add joist hangers for more support. If you can't use a full-depth hanger because of obstructions, use the next smaller size, such as a 2x4 joist hanger on a 2x6 joist.

When a joist has rotted or plumbers have cut through it to install a fixture or pipe, you can transfer its load to adjacent joists. Cut off the bad joist and nail a header across this cut end and into the neighboring joists, as you would when framing a stair opening. If the header has a span of 4 ft. or less, a single 2-by header will suffice.

Silencing Squeaky Floors

To fix a squeaky floor, you need to know why it squeaks. Underlayments and sub-floors may have loosened. The floor frame may be structurally inadequate. A wall may be improperly connected to a floor that spans a considerable distance and is flexing.

To fix loose wood flooring, drill small pilot-size holes ($3/32$ in. or so) down through the flooring or up through the subfloor and inject an epoxy adhesive. (The DriTac® wood floor repair kit includes epoxy and syringes for applying it.) If the floorboards have cupped or crowned, you may have moisture in the floor. Don't attempt a repair until you eliminate the moisture source. After warped flooring has dried thoroughly, the boards will usually regain their original shape and may need no repair. If you inject epoxy to re-adhere wood flooring, fill the pilot holes with putty and refinish. You also can use epoxy injection to reattach loose underlayment beneath resilient flooring.

When coming up with a remodeling plan, eye the ceilings as well as your walls. By removing a large segment of ceiling, this room now opens to a loft-like attic space.

Loose subfloors under a pile carpet are easy to fix with deck screws. Just run the screws through the carpet with a screw gun, and the heads will penetrate the padding and disappear. For carpets where the head of the screw would leave a visible mark, use a longer screw and stop before the head penetrates the carpet, leaving about an inch of shank showing. Use pliers to snap off the head. The Squeeeeek No More® Squeak Elimination Kit, manufactured by O'Berry Enterprises, makes this procedure easier with an alignment device, scored screws designed to break off beneath the surface of the flooring, and a rocker to shear off the screws.

Squeak-Ender® and Seam-Ender are repair kits designed to mechanically pull down subfloors that have buckled and attach them permanently to the joists. You should be able to find them at a home center.

Reinforcing an Attic Floor

You may find yourself adding a floor in the attic, adding a loft in a room with vaulted ceilings, or making practical use of the two-story foyer that modern builders have found so compelling. Adding floor area within the structure is one of the few remodeling investments that can yield a positive return right away—if you build economically.

Attic joists might be sufficient for supporting basic storage, but they generally are insufficient for living space. An obvious answer might be to *sister* deeper joists to the existing ones—that is, to double up joists. Stiffness is a matter of joist depth, not width, however, so deeper joists reduce headroom. By consulting a span table at the lumberyard, you can find the minimum joist depth and spacing for a stiffer floor. You may create a stiffer floor by reducing the spacing

Attics are tempting spaces to reclaim and remodel, but often the floors were not built to handle the loads typical of living areas. Remodeling an attic may entail beefing up the floors, as well as widening the stairway access and lifting the ceiling ties to obtain more headroom.

Hanging from a Beam

Although a beam usually works from underneath a load, in certain circumstances you can place the beam above and use joist hangers to attach the joists to it. This works best in attics where new walls can act as bridge girders to hold up the structure without having to lower the ceiling below. Often, spreading the load across the rafters is all you need to stiffen an otherwise structurally sufficient floor system.

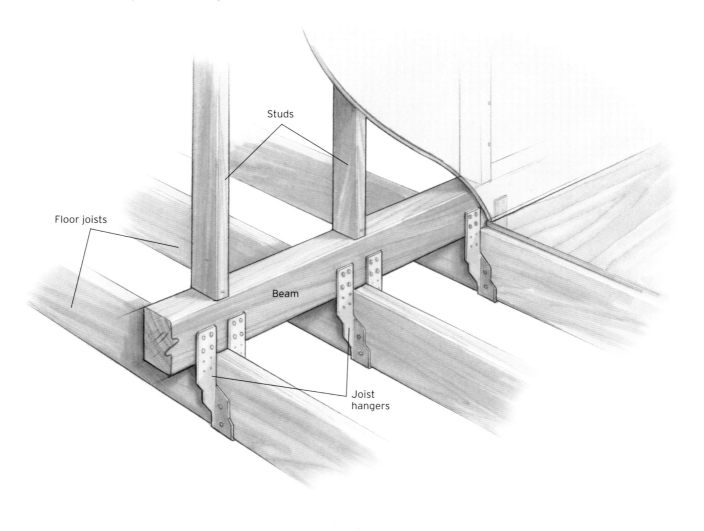

Studs

Floor joists

Beam

Joist hangers

WHEN IT COMES TO JOISTS, DEEPER IS BETTER. Spacing 2x10 joists 24 in. on center will provide a stronger and stiffer floor assembly than 2x8 joists of the same grade and species, spaced every 16 in.

between joists—for example, by setting 2x6 joists at 12-in. on center instead of 2x8 joists at 16-in. on center.

You can further stiffen a floor by adding a thick layer of subflooring, such as ¾-in. tongue-and-groove OSB floor sheathing that is glued and screwed to the joists. One builder I know uses a double layer of floor sheathing, with the second run perpendicular to the first, to strengthen attic floors without adding joists. However, a stiff, structurally sound floor can still bounce.

Another way to stiffen shallow attic joists is to add a beam on *top* of the joists. This solution works best if the beam coincides with a wall. Set an adequate-size beam—say a 4x10—perpendicular to and over the joists as close as possible to the middle of the span. Strap the floor joists to this beam with oversize joist hangers or the metal strapping used for framing. The beam will distribute the floor's loads across all the rafters for a much stiffer assembly.

Get the same results by strapping a new attic wall to the joists, so that instead of joists serving to support the walls, the walls act as a giant beam that braces the floor and spreads its load across the entire frame. Sheath the wall with drywall (or, for extra strength, ⅜-in. plywood sheathing), glued and screwed to the plates and studs.

Framing New Floors

If adding a new floor, you'll determine the appropriate framing sizes and spacing.

Deeper joists arranged with broader spacing provides maximum stiffness; 2x10 joists at 24 in. on center trumps 2x8 joists at 16 in.

I use 2x10s at 24 in. on center with ¾-in. tongue-and-groove OSB subflooring because it provides a good balance between high quality and low cost. Also, the larger joist bays provide more room for ducts and plumbing.

When choosing joist size, species, and spacing, calculate floor-framing requirements using actual occupancy loads: 40 pounds per square foot (psf) for living areas and 30 psf for bedrooms. Choose the least expensive of the joist wood species that will handle the load and span requirements of your layout. For example, if your joist spans allow you to use hem fir instead of Douglas fir, the savings can be substantial. If you can use SPF (spruce pine fir) instead of hem fir, you'll save even more. Study the options, make a materials list based on each, and ask the lumberyard to price them.

INSTALLING STAIRS

According to the rules of feng shui, you should handle the location of a stairwell very carefully or energy will escape through your front door and act as a financial drain on the household. Even if you don't gravitate toward the mystical approach to value engineering, stairwells can still consume many of your construction dollars if you don't plan well.

Photo courtesy of Easy Riser ®

Building a stairway from scratch is an involved, time-consuming project. The Easy Riser® system takes the mystery out of the job.

SAVING ON FRAMING

Simply by increasing joist spacing from 16 in. on center to 24 in., you can shave $75 to $100 off a typical remodel.

Lowered ceiling areas can change the atmosphere of a room or hallway, and they also have the very practical function of allowing you to conceal pipes and ducts or to recess lighting.

Whenever possible, locate stairs *parallel* to your floor framing to minimize structural changes. Where the stairway header remains within 3 ft. of the end of the joist span, and the width of the opening doesn't exceed 4 ft., you can frame the opening with single joists and headers without hangers.

If it's necessary to locate a stairwell *perpendicular* to the joists, place at least one side of the opening within 3 ft. of a girder or bearing wall so that you can end-nail tail joists (joists ending at a header) and avoid the time-consuming task of installing joist

hangers. The headers will require hangers, as will any tail joists more than 6 ft. in length.

Although it's traditional to build stairs with three stringers (the diagonal supports that run below the treads), stairs with a tread width of 36 in. or less need just two, as long as you limit the maximum run and rise to 4 ft. 6 in. and 4 ft., respectively. Most stairways span a full story, but you can avoid the third stringer by dividing the run into two segments with a landing or add a mid-span support wall.

Raise the Ceiling

Lifting the ceiling height can make a dramatic change in the appearance of a room. If your attic isn't quite big enough to turn into living space, consider raising a portion of the ceiling below.

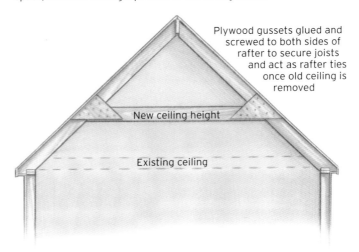

Plywood gussets glued and screwed to both sides of rafter to secure joists and act as rafter ties once old ceiling is removed

New ceiling height

Existing ceiling

DEALING WITH CEILINGS

An old house with tall ceilings in deteriorated condition is a candidate for a dropped ceiling, which can accommodate new mechanical and electrical systems. One approach is a suspended drywall system, which uses a metal channel attached to perimeter walls and metal studs suspended from wires attached to the ceiling framing. This spares you from having to construct a cumbersome dropped-ceiling structure with heavy, bulky wood framing. You hang drywall from the

An expedient way to drop hallway ceilings and create attractive architectural details is to use metal stud channel.

Dormer Styles

Dormers can turn dead attics into desirable living space while dressing up a plain roofline. And since they don't require new footings and involve only a minimal amount of framing, roofing, and siding, dormers can be a cost-effective remodel. Even if the attic isn't roomy enough to create living space, consider using a dormer at the top of a lightwell to bring sunlight into the rooms and stairways below.

Photo by Scott McBride

You can help keep framing costs down by building narrow dormers that can be accommodated within the existing rafter layout.

A gable dormer fits in nicely with a variety of architectural styles, including colonial, Tudor, and Craftsman. With a vaulted ceiling (no ceiling joists, just rafters), this dormer can open up the attic dramatically.

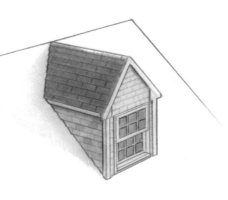

A hip dormer fits with prairie- or shingle-style houses. The narrow width makes it easier to frame within existing roof rafters. This dormer adds light but not much headroom.

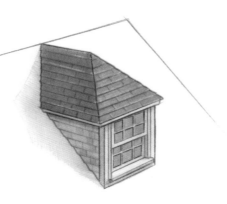

A shed dormer is the easiest to build, with uncomplicated framing. It can stretch nearly the full width of the roof to greatly expand the attic.

metal grid for a level, smooth ceiling that looks like the original, and at very low cost.

Raising the Ceiling

Although it's a somewhat unusual modification, you might consider *raising* the existing ceiling. There may be space in an unused portion of the attic, allowing you to remove ceiling joists and reinstall them a foot or more higher by attaching them to the raf-ters. When used in this way, ceiling joists act as rafter ties, preventing the weight of the roof from spreading the exterior wall of the home. So it's important to attach the joists firmly, using the plywood system illustrated on p. 73 or another structurally sound method. Consult with a building official or structural engineer to make sure the approach you choose is adequate to handling snow loads, wind, and other roof stresses.

Fire Sale Transformation

Ritch Paprocki bought a house for $25,000 at a fire sale. Besides its charred framing, the house was caked in soot, the windowpanes were cracked from the intense heat, and the smoky smell seemed impossible to remove.

Ritch replaced windows and most of the woodwork on the first floor, then removed walls to open up the kitchen to the dining room. The kitchen ceiling was dropped to define it as a separate space (as well as to hide plumbing for a new second-floor bathroom). The living room and parlor were small, and he joined them to make a great room while also reclaiming a pair of oak pillars to mark the entry foyer. And then he married Jodie. She moved in, and the remodeling continued.

By doing most of the work themselves and hiring out only the difficult parts of the project, the couple saved money as they sculpted a personal environment. "Buying power tools instead of hiring a contractor helped me save on the bigger projects and get the finishes I wanted," says Ritch. He was able to afford tiled kitchen countertops and gourmet kitchen appliances, purchased on a scratch-and-dent or closeout status. The farther in advance you plan, adds Ritch, "the more you can take advantage of bargain-bin items such as high-quality closeout doors, windows, cabinets, and flooring."

Before converting the attic into a master bedroom, Ritch Paprocki had to reframe the existing 2x4 ceiling joists with 2x10s.

4

Systems Tailoring

MOST HOMEOWNERS LEAVE IT UP TO THE PROS to decide how to run pipe, install central air-conditioning, and rope electrical systems. But a hands-off attitude can cost you when remodeling. This chapter explores alternative mechanical and electrical systems that make the job easier, give superior service, and save you money. We won't be looking at these components as stand-alone parts, but as gears in an integrated system—the machinery of your house.

This *whole-house* systems approach is an alternative to the old every-trade-for-itself method. It recognizes that separate building components can (and should) work toward the same end. For example, insulation, windows, exterior doors, heating, and air-conditioning are all related building components that should be considered together in striving for comfort,

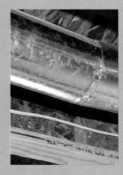

AN AVERAGE HOUSE MIGHT COST ABOUT $50 TO WEATHERIZE, but you can expect to save two to three times that much in energy savings in just one heating season.

long-term durability, and energy savings. If you upgrade your home's insulation and carefully follow simple air-sealing techniques, that in turn might mean being able to use a relatively small furnace or air-conditioning unit without sacrificing comfort. A well-sealed, well-insulated house typically uses about 25 percent less energy; money you save in summer as well as in winter.

Less obvious but no less important, plumbing and electrical systems are interdependent with window locations, fixture layouts, and room design. Practical, money-saving solutions are more likely to come to light if you and those helping you plan consider each part of the project as it relates to the others.

The structural, mechanical, and electrical systems of your house should be planned to work together as an integrated system, for ease of both installation and eventual repairs.

WEATHERPROOFING

I should confess that I once dismissed simple approaches to building challenges. As a hardheaded contractor, I thought the idea of using $30 worth of caulk and expanding foam sealant was a Band-Aid® approach to reducing fuel bills. My perspective changed when Bob Ruskamp, a local Energy Star® certifier and energy auditor, offered to perform a blower door test on my house. This procedure is something like a blood pressure test for a house. A technician mounts a fan on an exterior door to reduce

The tools for sealing a home are inexpensive and easy to use. Most of the work can be done with a caulking gun and tubes of expanding foam sealant.

PRO TIP

A WOOD-BURNING FIREPLACE MAY BE HEARTWARMING, but it actually has a cooling effect overall, potentially accounting for 15 percent of a home's heat loss. When not in use, the flue should be sealed off.

To track down the air leaks in your home, consider having a blower door test to create the effect of a 20-mph wind from all sides. You can detect leaks simply by feeling with your hand or holding up a stick of smoking incense.

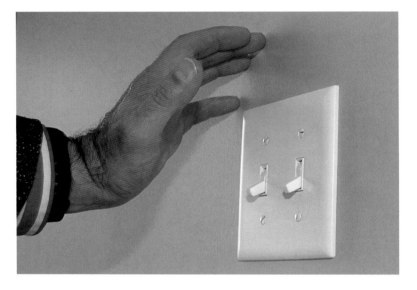

On a cold winter day, place your hand against a switch plate, on an interior wall, and you will learn firsthand how much air may leak into your house.

the pressure within the house, mimicking a 20-mph wind, and monitors how much air moves through the fan to determine how tight or leaky the construction is.

Nebraska was having a cold snap the day Bob set up his equipment on my front door. He inspected the house to make sure all the windows were closed, shut the fireplace flue, and turned off the furnace for safety. Finally, he turned on the fan and took a reading. "Better than most," he said, "but not good enough."

With the fan still on, Bob led me on a search for household air leaks. First came an obvious source. "Feel around this window," Bob said, and I placed my hand near the sash. An icy wind hit my palm. Then Bob cinched the window latch, and I felt a notable difference. "Lock your window sashes and the house will stay warmer," he said. Then I felt around the window trim and felt the wind

seeping around the casing. "You need to caulk and insulate these better," said Bob. I was surprised by our next stop. Bob asked me to place my hand near an electrical outlet on an interior wall. For me, the arctic draft blowing through the switch plate was a revelation.

As we moved from room to room, I felt the air leaking from plumbing pipe penetrations, light fixtures, dryer and bathroom vents, the fireplace flue, and even under the baseboards along exterior walls. I had thought of our brick house as sealed and solid, but now it seemed more like a billowing canvas tent. It was clear to me now why my heating bills were so high: Excellent levels of insulation don't take the place of air sealing.

I tightened up our house, carefully sealing the window frames, holes made for plumbing and wiring, and the lines where the floor meets the exterior walls. When Bob returned, his blower door test revealed a

78   AFFORDABLE REMODEL

FOR A QUICK-AND-DIRTY CALCULATION of just how much you would save by reducing air leaks and upgrading insulation, deduct 30 percent from your yearly utility costs.

PRO TIP

Attics tend to be riddled with holes to feed electrical cables, pipes, and ducts. Collectively, the holes in the average home admit as much outside air as a wide-open window. Seal these with fire-rated caulk.

much tighter structure. Another test was our monthly fuel bills, which dropped by about $50 a month. In terms of cost and effectiveness, sealing and insulation come first, followed by air-conditioning upgrades and then storm or replacement windows.

Secrets of Successful Sealing

It helps to picture air infiltration as water, seeping into your house through small leaks. You'd lose no time in fixing these leaks, but air infiltration is much less likely to get your attention.

Attics are the leakiest parts of houses. They typically have large openings for ventilation and yet aren't sealed off from the living space below. You may have insulation in the attic, but that doesn't mean it is *air sealed*. Picture yourself standing in a winter storm with a wool sweater but no windbreaker. That's what's going on under your roof. Attic

insulation lowers thermal transfer, like a sweater, but it has little effect on moving air. Cold air blows right through it, and there are probably leaks through recessed ceiling lights, bathroom fans, plumbing, wiring, and ceiling registers in your house right now. Meanwhile, warm household air rises in what is known as the chimney effect, exiting leaks in the structure's envelope as it trades places with cold outside air.

It's especially important to plug holes between the attic and the rooms below. Begin by shutting off the power at the appropriate circuit breakers. Remove ceiling light fixtures, registers, and bathroom fan covers and caulk the spaces between them and the drywall. If the attic is unfinished, make sure the power is off and pull back the insulation surrounding the places where plumbing and wiring penetrate the top plate of the walls below. Seal the holes with caulk or expanding foam

For a warm and weather-tight wall, run insulation along the band joist and apply blown cellulose on the wall below.

IF YOU HAVE RECESSED LIGHTS IN AN ATTIC CEILING, make sure they are the sealed variety. Better yet, don't install recessed lights in attic ceilings, because even the best units allow warm air to escape like small chimneys.

Caulk around ceiling boxes to prevent warmed household air from venting up into an unheated attic.

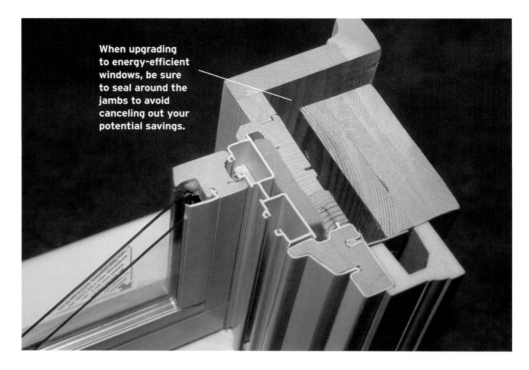

When upgrading to energy-efficient windows, be sure to seal around the jambs to avoid canceling out your potential savings.

sealant. If there's enough space for the tip of the caulk cartridge or the nozzle of the foam sealant, also plug the holes (called knock-outs) where wires enter junction boxes.

Next, with the power off, remove electrical wall plates for switches and outlets and install thin foam gaskets to stop infiltration. Even outlet safety caps, designed for child-proofing, will do their part to block drafts.

If you feel up to it, remove the trim around windows and exterior doors and spray a low-volume foam sealant into the gap between the jambs and the framing. Don't use standard foam because it may expand so much that it bends the jambs and causes window and doors to bind.

Another key area to seal is along the band joist in the basement. This is the board that

sits upright on top of the foundation around the perimeter of the house. Caulk the seam between the rim joist and the floor sheathing above, between the rim joist and the sill plate that lies flat below, and between the sill plate and the foundation. More effective for this difficult-to-reach area is to have an insulation company spray foam along these joints.

Attic Insulation

Once you've finished sealing, consider adding insulation if the existing levels don't meet current code. To know for sure, call your local building department and ask for the minimum attic and wall insulation requirements. The ratings will be in terms of *R-value,* representing resistance to heat flow. To determine the R-value of the existing

Sealing the Envelope

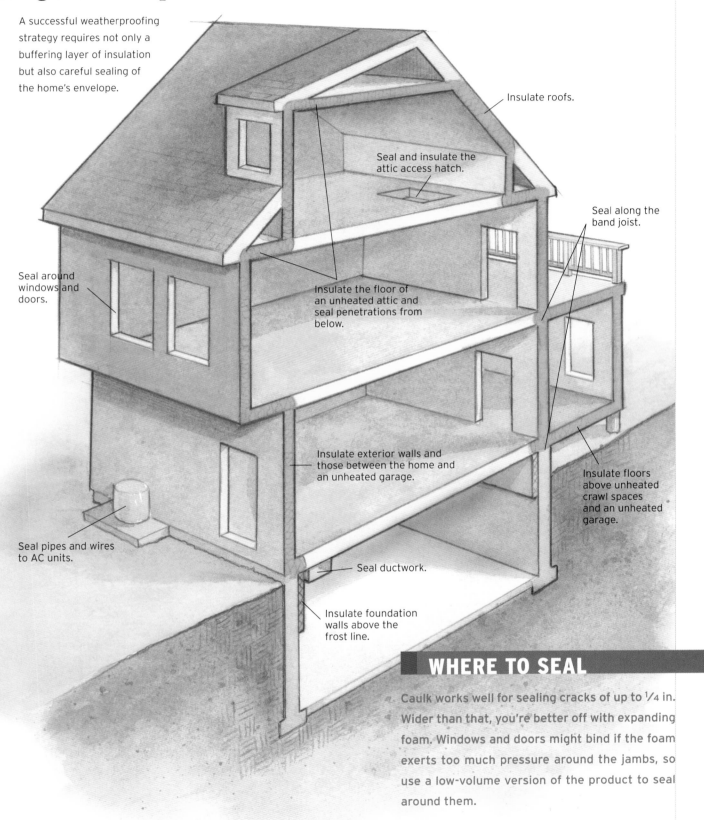

A successful weatherproofing strategy requires not only a buffering layer of insulation but also careful sealing of the home's envelope.

Insulate roofs.

Seal and insulate the attic access hatch.

Seal along the band joist.

Seal around windows and doors.

Insulate the floor of an unheated attic and seal penetrations from below.

Insulate exterior walls and those between the home and an unheated garage.

Insulate floors above unheated crawl spaces and an unheated garage.

Seal pipes and wires to AC units.

Seal ductwork.

Insulate foundation walls above the frost line.

WHERE TO SEAL

Caulk works well for sealing cracks of up to 1/4 in. Wider than that, you're better off with expanding foam. Windows and doors might bind if the foam exerts too much pressure around the jambs, so use a low-volume version of the product to seal around them.

Foundation Weatherproofing

The top of the foundation is apt to be one of the leakiest areas of the home and also one of the most frequently overlooked.

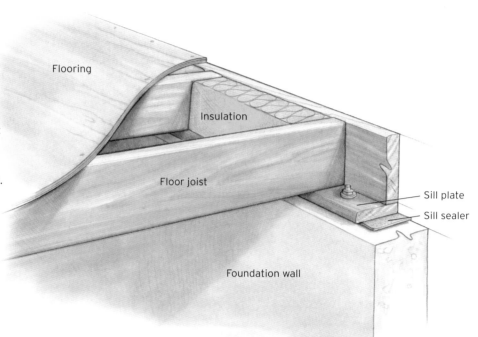

Flooring

Insulation

Floor joist

Sill plate

Sill sealer

Foundation wall

CAULK CHOICES

Not all caulks are created equal. **Latex** and **acrylic** products are easy to use, and they clean up with water. They'll hold up better if painted and work best on cracks that won't expand and contract more than $1/8$ in. **Silicone** caulk is a more durable choice, and it adheres better. But it sets up very quickly, and you can't wash it off with water, making cleanup a challenge. It's the best type of caulk for metal and glass, but paint cannot stick to some silicone products. Either paint before caulking or buy a silicone product labeled as paintable.

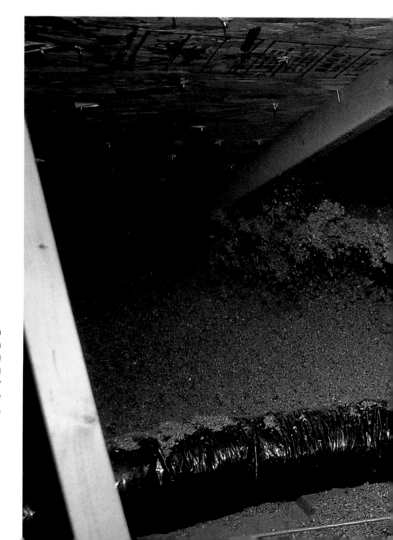

A small investment in upgraded attic insulation not only will save you money in the long run, but will make your house more comfortable right away.

fiberglass batts, measure their thickness with a ruler. The chart below gives the R-values for various thicknesses. Add more insulation if you have 6 in. or less. Even if you find you have 9½ in., or the equivalent of R-30, you may want to add a layer of unfaced R-19 batts across the joists. This is likely to do more to keep your house warm in winter than upgrading the furnace, and at a much lower cost.

Wall Insulation

To determine what sort of insulation you have in your exterior walls, take a peek. Turn off the power to the room at the service panel, then remove the cover plate of an outlet and probe with a stick. If you find no insulation whatsoever, consider hiring an insulation company to blow in cellulose or fiberglass. This is accomplished by drilling holes between studs through either the inside or the outside of your house (depending on whether you'd rather patch and paint interior walls or your siding) and then blowing insulation into the cavity. The procedure isn't foolproof, because wires, pipes, and wood blocking within the walls can make it difficult to fill the cavities completely. If the walls already have some insulation, it may not be worth your while to try to improve the R-value.

An easier way to make your home more comfortable is to roll on a layer of radiant barrier paint. In winter, interior walls will absorb less of the heat generated in the house; in summer, exterior walls will reflect heat

Blown-in cellulose insulation will fill in around uneven framing and electrical boxes, making it an excellent choice for remodeling projects. You can blow in cellulose before putting up drywall or by making holes in the existing wall surface.

R-VALUE OF FIBERGLASS BATTS BY THICKNESS

Fiberglass batts are a popular form of insulation for do-it-yourselfers because they are easy to install, although the skin and lungs should be protected.

R-VALUE	THICKNESS (INCHES)
R-38	12
R-30	9 ½ to 10
R-25	8
R-19	6 to 6 ½
R-15	3
R-13	3
R-11	3 ½

THE INSULATION ON BASEMENT WALLS DOESN'T NEED TO EXTEND below the frost level. If the local frost depth is 36 in., you have to insulate only that far below the soil line. The earth below frost depth remains at about 55°F year-round.

High-density foam board is a good choice for insulating basement walls. It is relatively easy to install and impervious to moisture.

from outdoors. The best place to apply the paint depends on where you live. If you are in a cold climate, use it on the inside surface of the exterior walls of the house and on ceilings below the attic. If you live in a warm region, use the paint on the outside surface of the exterior walls. If you can't find radiant-barrier paint in a color you like, you can get the same reflective effect by mixing a ceramic-based paint additive with standard paint.

Basement walls are often overlooked when it comes to insulating. If the walls are unfinished (if you can see exposed concrete), consider installing 1½-in. panels of rigid foam insulation directly to the surface using construction adhesive. Make sure the adhesive is compatible, because some products will eat through the insulation. Check the manufacturer's recommendations for a suitable product.

Although foam insulation is hard to ignite, it burns quickly and emits toxic smoke. So panels should be covered with laminated insulation board that has a fire-resistant foil facing or with drywall.

If you have uneven stone foundation walls, an insulation company can blow nonflammable cellulose insulation onto the surface. Mixed with adhesives, the insulation stays in place and dries stiff to the touch. The result isn't particularly beautiful, but it will be a relatively inexpensive means of lowering your fuel bill.

Housewrap

A major remodeling may provide the opportunity to improve the weather barrier around your home. And although sealing

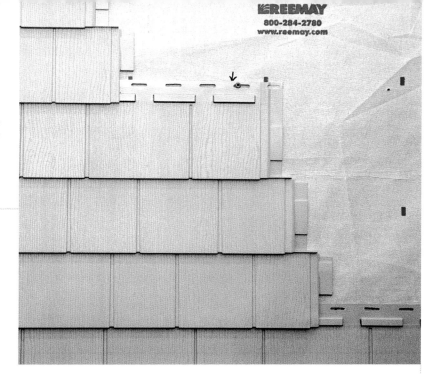

If your remodeling plans call for replacing siding, don't forget the housewrap. This layer not only will keep framing dry but also will stop wind from blowing through the walls.

an existing house typically presents a bigger challenge than doing the same for a new one, even limited improvement can significantly lower energy consumption.

Roofing and siding are the first-line water barriers. Behind them, traditional felt paper (a.k.a. *tar paper*) or the newer *housewraps* act as secondary moisture barriers. Felt paper has its strengths. It seals itself when penetrated by nails and staples and is inexpensive. The more expensive housewrap is a fabric mesh that keeps out wind and water but is porous enough for water vapor to escape. If trapped, vapor can cause framing to decay and foster mold growth, which affects indoor air quality. While I don't recommend removing siding just to install housewrap, if you are re-siding, you might replace the existing felt with a layer of Typar® or Tyvek®.

SAVE ON HEATING AND COOLING

Once you've sealed and insulated your home, contact an energy consultant for a complete energy assessment. Some utility companies provide this service free. Otherwise, look in the phone book or use the Internet to contact the Residential Energy Services Network (RESNET), which maintains a state-by-state list of certified consultants. A consultation involves reviewing insulation levels, window efficiency, wall-to-window ratios, heating and cooling system efficiency, solar orientation, and the water-heating system. The consultant can conduct a blower door test as well as a duct-blaster test to uncover any leakage in the home's ducts.

If you will be replacing siding as part of a remodeling project, now is your chance to conscientiously flash and seal your home against water and wind.

With the help of an energy consultant, you can improve the comfort of your home, save on energy costs, and save still more by purchasing smaller heating and cooling systems.

The consultant will come up with a balanced, cost-effective strategy that may include upgrading your windows and adding insulation. Those changes should reduce your energy bills and allow you to buy a smaller heating and cooling system that, over time, will help offset the cost of those improvements. I always ask the energy consultant to give me several combinations of insulation, window, and systems recommendations to mull over with cost estimates in hand.

A consultant certified as a Home Energy Rating System (HERS) rater can translate your home's performance into a score recognized by the home mortgage industry. This rating might allow you to borrow more money or to qualify for certain tax incentives.

Selecting New Heating Equipment

When replacing a heating system, you stand to save money by taking advantage of the existing ductwork and wiring. Here are some questions to get started:

■ If central air-conditioning isn't needed, could a hot-water system or a radiant-heating

TRADE SECRET
ENERGY INCENTIVES

Energy-sparing options will reduce long-term operational expenses, but they can add substantial up-front costs to a remodeling project. One way to offset the cost of upgraded mechanical systems, energy-efficient windows, insulation, and solar water heaters is to take advantage of tax and utility incentives. Many utility companies offer fuel credits and even cash incentives for upgrading your furnace and air-conditioning. Some states provide tax incentives for such alternative energy products as photovoltaic systems and wind generators.

Unlike the solar panels of yesteryear, today's low-profile systems are barely visible from the street. This house derives all of its electricity and hot water from the sun.

system meet your needs instead of forced-air heat?

■ If you want air-conditioning as well as heating, is a heat pump practical for your home? A heat pump requires the expense of a special circuit for the pump itself and low-voltage wiring for the thermostat.

■ If you need to cool your home but don't want central air-conditioning, could a room air conditioner, evaporative cooler, or duct-less mini-split system meet your needs? If so, consider heating and air-conditioning options separately.

■ Do you want to make use of solar energy to heat or cool your home?

Choosing Your Fuel

Your utility costs may influence whether you choose an electric, natural gas, propane, or fuel oil heating system. An electric system costs the least to install because there is no need for flues or piping. In certain areas of the country, electric rates remain low enough that this equipment, when com-bined with a high-efficiency heat pump, can

be economical in the long run. And when gas and fuel oil prices climb in anticipa-tion of a severe winter, owners of all-electric homes have the advantage. On the other hand, electric rates may go up and reverse the balance.

One solution is to install a dual-fuel hybrid system that lets you change from gas to electric with the flip of a switch. If you live in a moderate climate where tem-peratures usually remain above freezing and electric rates are reasonable, this may be the most efficient way to heat and cool. When the temperature is above 35°F or so, the sys-tem uses electricity for heating. Below that, a backup furnace uses gas as a supplemental source. A dual-fuel unit costs about $600 to $1,000 more than a conventional heating system, but you should make back that amount after two to three years through lower heating costs. Because these systems help utilities balance their peak demand periods, some companies offer financing or cash incentives to help offset purchase and installation costs.

A heat pump can both heat and cool by reversing the direction of the refrigerant in the system. Although it costs a few hundred dollars more than a standard air conditioner, a heat pump can cut utility bills in temperate climates.

Photo by Larry Douglas

An electric furnace provides a cost-effective back-up system for a heat pump in regions where coal generation affords cheaper kilowatts.

INVEST IN THE ENVELOPE

An energy consultant can prepare a table showing you how much you stand to save in equipment and annual fuel costs by upgrading your sealing and insulation. Here is an example for a typical 2,000-sq.-ft. house.

AREA	MATERIAL	TYPE	UPGRADE	ADDED UPGRADE COST
Walls	Cellulose	R-13	R-15	$75
Ceiling (flat)	Blown-in	R-30	R-45	$65
Ceiling (vaulted)	Batt	R-30	R-45	$100
Top of foundation	Spray foam	R-11	R-19	$75
Windows		Double glazed	Low-e with argon gas	$150
Heating		32,347 BTU	24,163 BTU	($250)
Heat pump		2 ton	1.5 ton	($250)
NET COST DIFFERENCE FOR UPGRADE				SAVINGS OF $35
NET COST DIFFERENCE IN ENERGY USE				SAVINGS OF $75 ANNUALLY

HEATING AND COOLING EFFICIENCY

Efficiency ratings vary greatly with the type of fuel and the technology of the equipment.

FUEL AND EQUIPMENT	AVERAGE EFFICIENCY (PERCENT)
OIL	
High-efficiency central heating	89.0
Typical central heating	80.0
Water heater (50 gal.)	59.5
GAS	
High-efficiency central furnace	97.0
Typical central boiler	85.0
Minimum-efficiency central furnace	78.0
Room heater, unvented	99.0
Room heater, vented	65.0
Water heater (50 gal.)	62.0
ELECTRICITY	
Baseboard, resistance	99.0
Central heating, forced air	97.0
Central heating, heat pump	200+
Ground source heat pump	300+
Water heater (50 gal.)	97.0
WOOD AND PELLETS	
Franklin stoves	30.0 to 40.0
Stoves with circulating fans	40.0 to 70.0
Catalytic stoves	65.0 to 75.0
Pellet stoves	85.0 to 90.0

MONEY OUT THE WINDOW

According to the American Council for an Energy Efficient Economy, each year in the United States nearly $13 billion worth of energy escapes through holes and cracks in homes in the form of heated or cooled air. If that statistic is hard to believe, consider that a 1/16-in. crack around a window can let in as much cold air as leaving the window open 3 in.

Some Alternatives for Keeping Warm

Another frugal way of heating your home is with the water heater. Specialized gas models will take care of space heating while warming up the household water. Known as a combination (or combo) system, this approach makes sense for small houses in moderate climates. You save money because a single appliance performs two functions, with only one gas line and vent.

The combo system circulates hot water through a heat exchanger, and a blower moves the heated air through a standard duct system. In the summer, an air-conditioner connected to the exchanger pushes cool air through the ductwork. The use of gas water heaters is generally considered an environmentally positive (although not perfect) choice, especially if you use a model with 90 percent efficiency. Some heaters can be vented through the wall with PVC pipe instead of up a galvanized metal flue, making installation simpler. As a final advantage, combo systems take up a lot less space than a pair of separate systems, making them a good choice if you are trying to squeeze a few extra inches out of your house.

SIZE MATTERS IN AIR-CONDITIONING

In our first house, I installed the largest air-conditioning system available. It was a 5-ton mammoth for a 1,600-sq.-ft. house and, I thought, money well spent. We could cool the house quickly, but within a half hour we were uncomfortably cold, the thermostat shut down the system and the house became clammy.

The problem caused by an oversize air-conditioning system is that it lowers the temperature before it lowers the humidity to a comfortable level. A properly sized air-conditioning system runs longer, dehumidifying the air as it works to maintain the temperature. This is good from a cost perspective, because you can use a smaller, less-expensive system and it improves comfort. To determine the proper size for your BTU requirements, ask an energy consultant or a competent heating and air-conditioning contractor to do a heat-gain/heat-loss calculation. Do not give in to the temptation to upgrade by installing an unsightly larger unit. The basic calculations which take into account the "tightness" of your exterior shell already have a built-in safety factor.

Finally, an oversize system costs more to operate. Air-conditioners are least efficient when first starting, and smaller units hum along for extended periods without shutting on and off.

Arid Alternatives

In a dry climate, you might consider an evaporative cooler, also known as a swamp cooler. It cools things down in the way that sweating keeps you from overheating. The idea came out of an old custom: In the days before air-conditioning, people would sleep outside on a screened porch hung with damp sheets. As the night wind blew through the sheets, the vaporizing water absorbed some of the heat.

Following this principle, an evaporative cooler uses a fan to pull outside air through moist, absorbent material, which makes air entering the house as much as 30°F cooler— for about a quarter of the energy it takes to run an air conditioner. Unlike air-conditioning, which recirculates the same air, a cooler brings in fresh air, raising its humidity somewhat. Its evaporative function is suited only to dry and desertlike air and becomes less effective as the humidity rises.

Evaporative coolers are less expensive than air-conditioning units and easier to install. What's more, utilities may offer substantial rebates for installing a ducted evaporative cooler. On a new system, a short duct directs the cooled air to a central point in the house. From there, you can direct the air through the various rooms by simply opening and closing doors and windows.

When sizing an air-conditioning system, its capacity has to be just right. If the unit is too big, it will lower temperatures but fail to adequately dehumidify the air; if it is too small, the equipment won't be able to keep up on a hot day.

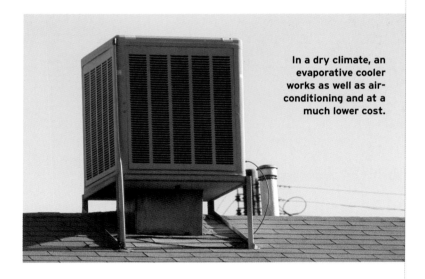

In a dry climate, an evaporative cooler works as well as air-conditioning and at a much lower cost.

SIZING A SWAMP COOLER

The proper size for a swamp cooler depends not only on the home's square footage but also on the climate. A unit's evaporative effect will work best in moderate, dry weather.

COOLER CAPACITY	MODERATE DRY CLIMATE	HOT DRY CLIMATE
3,000 cfm per	1,000 sq. ft.	750 sq. ft.
3,500 cfm per	1,165 sq. ft.	875 sq. ft.

WHEN PACKING FOR A VACATION, DON'T FORGET THE THERMOSTAT. Most newer models have a vacation setting that allows you to scale back energy use for the time you will be away. Once you're back home, you can restore your normal settings with the push of a button.

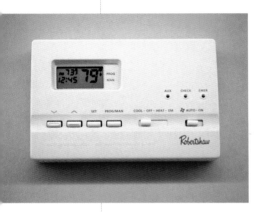

Thermostats have come a long way from the simple dial-up kind, allowing you to customize settings in a number of ways.

THERMOSTATS: LOCATION, LOCATION, LOCATION

The location of the thermostat can make all the difference in whether a system will keep you comfortable. Set it upstairs by the bedrooms, and chances are the first floor will be cold on winter mornings. Place it by the front door, and every time you open the door you'll hear the fan come on to fight off the resulting gust of cold or hot outside air. Place it near a fireplace (as we did), and whenever you cozy up by the hearth the rest of your house will freeze. Generally, a central location away from exterior doors and heat sources will be the happiest compromise.

A programmable, computerized thermostat can make the most of your energy dollars, especially if you learn how to use the thing. It not only reads temperature but works like a timer, allowing you to program a weekly cycle with settings at various temperature points throughout the day. For example, I set my thermostat at 78°F on summer nights and at 80°F during the day. On weekends, the day setting begins at 9 a.m., when most of the family climbs out of bed, but during the workweek, it moves to 7 a.m. In winter, the settings become more elaborate, with temperatures set on a seven-day cycle that accommodates school hours Monday through Friday, Saturday-night parties, and lazy, late-rising Sundays. We used to fiddle with the thermostat throughout the day, but now we adjust it just twice a year.

Another option, especially useful in remodeling situations, is the wireless thermostat. You can try various spots around the house with it until you find the best spot to ensure overall comfort. Then mount the thermostat on the wall and never move it.

DUCTING

If you plan to change out your heating and air-conditioning equipment, try to use the existing ductwork. Installing larger ducts is expensive and requires lots of cutting, framing, and patching. Instead, thoroughly seal and insulate your house so that less air volume is needed to maintain a comfortable temperature. When adding ducts to a new area of the house, keep them within the

SMART THERMOSTATS

The new programmable thermostats are a little like old VCRs, full of features that few people learn to use. But these thermostats can save you money, and it's worth cracking open the owner's manual and learning how to operate the things. Most thermostats will allow you to set a seven-day cycle, adjusting temperatures for when you're asleep, away at work, or home for the weekend. Most come with an economical away mode, which keeps the temperature just above freezing and just below sweltering while you're away. Some even tell you when it's time to change the system's air filter.

Ducts should be installed in a chase within the conditioned space of the house instead of passing through an unconditioned attic, crawl space, or basement.

conditioned envelope so that they won't be vulnerable to outside temperature extremes.

If you're adding air-conditioning to a house that's more than 25 years old, you may discover that the ducts aren't large enough to distribute the volume of air you need. You can get around this, to a degree, by adding new distribution ducts in key areas, such as the far end of the house or the second floor. Unlike heating, air-conditioning requires circulation because cold air tends to stratify near the floor and will not cool the house evenly unless properly blended (heat, on the other hand, requires less thorough mixing of the air to warm your house).

To churn the air and allow it to circulate out of the rooms, undercut doors or create a transom-like opening between rooms and the hallway, which is where most central air returns are located. Ironically, houses 40 to 50 years old usually have larger ducts than newer homes and these work best for retro-fitted central air-conditioning. Old-timers tended to oversize the ducting for heat systems because they lacked knowledge about forced-air dynamics. Later, they corrected this, making their ducts smaller—and then when air-conditioning became popular, the ducts became large again.

LEAKY DUCTS

Regardless of the duct size, they work best when they don't leak. You don't accept leaky water pipes, yet most ductwork is full of holes that spill precious conditioned air into the attic, wall cavities, and basement. Holes get poked in ducts by nails, and the joints

If you rely on ducts to distribute conditioned air through your house, you may face the challenge of finding ways to accommodate new runs when remodeling.

The black band shown here is a canvas coupling that can be added to ductwork to prevent the furnace fan's mechanical chatter from rattling ducts throughout the house.

between sections of ductwork loosen and open over time. But, oddly, the remedy is *not* duct tape, which performs poorly. Instead, use foil tape or duct mastic to seal ductwork permanently.

For sealing ducts, mastic tends to work best and to last longest. But it's impractical for sealing the ducts hidden inside your walls. An alternative to mastic is to use an advanced technique for sealing ducts that was developed at the Lawrence Berkeley National labs. Instead of wrapping or caulking individual joints, technicians pressurize existing ductwork using an aerosol sealant. This technique plugs leaks in air ducts effectively. By using this system on your old ducts, you end up with fewer leaks than if you had applied the best mastic to a new ductwork installation. The average savings from duct sealing exceeds $300 a year; it costs about $1,000 to have the work done on an average-size home.

Ductless Systems

Today, air-conditioning systems exist that don't need any ductwork. Mini-split systems use individual cooling units, placed room by room, and require only a thin refrigerant and power line connecting them to an outdoor air-conditioning compressor and fan. Hotels often use these systems, which you can expand over time by adding rooms as the need arises. This provides a means of heating and cooling a newly remodeled area without incurring the great expense of running ductwork from the existing system. In cases where the system is too small and would be over-taxed by serving the added living area, the mini-split affords an economical and convenient solution.

Another solution, known as a high-velocity system, uses 2-in. insulated air-supply tubing to deliver chilled air. Because the micro-ducts are flexible and of a small diameter, you can snake these hose-like ducts through existing

Unsealed joints between ducts will allow conditioned air to leak en route, meaning you are delivering less cool or warm air to the rooms that need it.

If you can't find the room for standard ductwork when adding central air, look into using high-velocity, small-diameter ducts instead.

Photo courtesy of Unico, Inc., and Newport Partners

2x4 walls to deliver forced air where needed. The registers are unobtrusive and resemble recessed lights more than the standard heating/air-conditioning registers you're probably familiar with. High-velocity systems represent the latest, high-tech heating and air-conditioning alternative, costing more than a regular duct installation, but saving money in old homes through the reduced need for rough carpentry, patching, drywall, and subsequent finish work. The systems are also very quiet, which makes them ideal for media rooms. Besides delivering cold air, they can also pump clean, filtered warm air during the winter months.

Fireplaces

Although fireplaces evoke warmth and comfort, many actually waste energy by sending warm air up through the flue and to the outside. As much as 15 percent of the heat energy in a typical house can escape

WHEN IS A HOUSE TOO TIGHT?

It's difficult to make a house too tight, given the many possible points of air infiltration. But your home may not have sufficient ventilation if you have an old furnace or gas water heater that puts out carbon monoxide, if high humidity isn't vented through exhaust fans, or if you live in an area troubled by radon gas. A certified energy auditor can ensure the minimum recommended ventilation for your particular climate zone and household size.

THE NUMBER OF BLADES IN A FAN IS UNIMPORTANT. In fact, some of the most effective fans only have two. A more important consideration is the pitch, or angle, of the blades. To move a good volume of air, look for blades with a pitch of at least 12 degrees.

through the chimney on a cold winter day. The exception comes with high-efficiency gas fireplaces; wood, pellet, corn kernel stoves (all of which used sealed combustion chambers); and certain electric fireplaces.

If you want to burn for heat (rather than just for atmosphere), a traditional wood stove, or the depression-era invention, the corn stove, would provide the best alternatives over a traditional fireplace. For the sake of comparison, it would cost about $125 a month to heat a 2,000-sq.-ft. home with wood, $130 a month with corn, and $247 for natural gas. Like the kernel stove, a super-efficient pellet stove is also one of the cleanest-burning options. These burn pellets formed from wood waste. A thermostat-controlled auger delivers fuel from a hopper to the firebox. Fans pull air in and exhaust gases out through a house-warming heat exchanger. Pellet stoves use electricity for the fan and need battery backup to operate during power outages. A quality stove will cost between $2,000 and $3,000 installed, comparable to a wood- or gas-burning fireplace.

The least expensive fireplace to install, especially if you are using it to create atmosphere and not to heat your home, is the electric fireplace. Don't wince, the new electric units look very realistic and actually throw off heat. Also, you can install them virtually anywhere in the house without the need for venting. Costing about two-thirds the cost of a gas unit, the newest electric models require their own 20-amp electric circuit, but no gas lines or flues. They are also very compact, fitting into spaces that a wood- burning or gas fireplace might not fit.

Gas fireplaces are more flexible than their wood-burning cousins because, although they require a flue to vent exhaust gasses and an outside air intake for combustion, the size of these flues are considerably smaller and can handle almost right-angle installations, which make it possible to install a gas-burning stove in the center of a room and then vent it out through the adjacent wall (rather that through the roof as is usually the case). One type of gas-burning fireplace, the ventless variety, promises the same level of flexibility as the electric units but with a more realistic-looking flame.

Not all code jurisdictions allow this type of fireplace because of the concern that a malfunction could lead to a deadly buildup of carbon monoxide in the air inside the house. If you install any kind of gas-burning stove, vented or ventless, it's a good idea to have a carbon monoxide detector.

Ceiling Fans

In your efforts to upgrade, don't forget about ceiling fans. In summer, their cooling effect allows you to raise the thermostat by about 4°F. In winter, with the blades turning slowly in reverse (toward the ceiling), a fan pushes warm air down from the ceiling to maintain even temperatures.

When I install fans, I pick rooms where the family prefers to congregate as well as hot spots, such as sunrooms and kitchens. Fans balance temperatures by keeping hot and cool air from stratifying, and they also help distribute warm air from a fireplace or passive solar windows throughout the home.

Ceiling fans not only look attractive but also can work as an integral and economical part of your air-conditioning and heating system.

Most PEX installations include a central distribution manifold, which works a lot like an electrical breaker box to provide a single location for all shutoffs.

PLUMBING WITH PEX

1. Cut the tube squarely with a sharp blade in a special PEX cutting tool.

2. Slip a steel collar over the tube, then insert a barbed brass connector into it.

3. Squeeze the collar with the proprietary crimpling tool, and you're done.

PEX plastic pipe has become a low-cost, easily installed alternative to copper.

ALTERNATIVE PLUMBING PRODUCTS

It's easy to convince people to embrace new approaches to heating and air-conditioning, but they typically are indifferent to advances in plumbing. So, here is a brief rundown of innovations you might consider for your remodeling.

Flexible Plumbing

Flexible cross-linked polyethylene (PEX) water pipe is a great convenience when remodeling. It snakes through wood framing with ease and provides a leak-free, joint-free conduit for water throughout the house. The pipe can be pulled from one location to another, so that you won't have to patch as many—or even any—walls after the plumber runs a line to new fixtures. Flexible line also expands greatly before cracking, which makes it more reliable in cold climates. Even though PEX requires special tools and training to install, it shaves about a third off labor time.

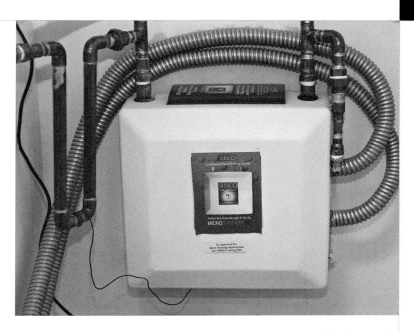

SAVE WATER AND YOU'LL SAVE ELECTRICITY.
That's because reduced water consumption will mean less
work for your water heater. The bonus is water bill savings.

PRO TIP

Air-admittance valves come in three sizes, from small units like the one pictured, adequate to vent a single bathroom, to a large vertical stack sufficient for an entire house.

A tankless water heater takes up little room and is a good choice in homes where space is very tight.

Ventless Drain Lines

Home plumbing systems include vents to exhaust sewer gas and to allow atmospheric pressure into the system to push wastewater down the drain. It can take a lot of pipe to find a path from every fixture group to the roof, and that adds up to a challenge if a remodeling project involves new plumbing.

Enter *air-admittance valves,* a code-approved, recognized technology that can allow you to skip the vent-through-the-roof system. Check with your building inspector to see if they are approved for use in your area. These valves greatly simplify matters by opening when a plumbing fixture is discharged, temporarily allowing atmospheric pressure into the line and preventing the escape of ozone-depleting sewer gases.

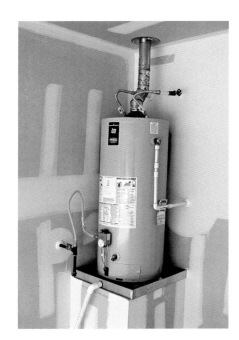

This old storage-tank water heater should look familiar to you and to your grandfather. But the rest of the world has moved on, and outside the United States, most water heater systems have no tank.

WATER HEATERS

When you think of a water heater, you probably picture a big storage tank sitting in a utility closet or basement corner. This tank-type heater is by far the most common

type in the United States. While relatively inexpensive to install, it loses heat (and wastes energy) because hot water sits in the tank until a tap is turned on, and then it travels through the pipes. In other countries, tankless heaters are the norm. They heat water via a series of heating coils and are known as demand systems because the coils heat up only when hot water is needed. They are more energy efficient and provide a continuous flow of hot water—you never run out, even with teens in the house. They are particularly suited to homes with natural gas, because an electric tankless model often requires an electric panel upgrade.

Solar water heating makes sense in climates with lots of sunlight. The units now on the market are considerably less expensive and more reliable than earlier models.

ELECTRICAL SYSTEM

If you plan to extensively remodel an older house, the existing panel may not be able to handle the added load of new appliances and lighting fixtures, which means you probably want to upgrade the electrical system. A benefit of upgrading is that it may afford you the opportunity to add an energy-efficient heat pump, with the resulting savings helping offset the cost of the electrical work.

You don't necessarily have to replace all of the wiring. It's possible to continue using the existing panel and wiring as a subsystem of a new one, so that the existing distribution of circuits is not affected by adding new ones..

Lighting Considerations

The matter of lighting is usually an afterthought in the remodeling process. While you can get by with an electrician's advice on what to install and where, you might consult with a lighting designer when revamping your wiring scheme. You'll learn about novel lighting systems and how they can best work in your home.

Along with the standard ambient light required by code, you should consider other types of lighting. *Decorative* lights can be a feature all to themselves and can be used to create a mood. *Task* lighting is for work areas, such as above the kitchen sink. *Focal* lighting illuminates art or architectural details. And *safety* lighting allows you to clearly see stairways, pathways, and exits. By mixing these, you will have better lighting and lower electric bills, because not every square foot of the home has to be brilliantly lit.

When planning a lighting system, there's a tendency to add too many switches. A complex bank of wall switches can be more of an annoyance than a convenience. Instead, consider using dimmers to adjust lighting for assorted activities, such as low light for watching television and bright light for reading.

Of course, the least expensive light is sunlight, so explore ways your remodeling project can better use daylight. Beyond standard windows, you might think about using tube skylights above halls and bathrooms, glass block, and transoms over doorways. Artificial lighting can account for between 10 percent and 25 percent of a home's energy use, so relying on the sun potentially will make a difference in your electric bills.

You can avoid fishing wire from wall outlets to new ceiling light fixtures by installing lights high up along the wall. Use lights with built-in switches, or connect the lights to a switched outlet.

Track lighting is a cinch to add when remodeling if there is a junction box in the ceiling. The track allows you to place pendant lights, spots, or even a chandelier exactly where you want it.

Photo by: William Asdal

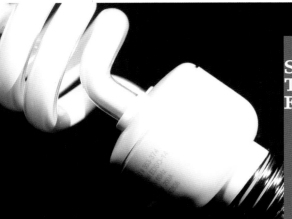

Nowadays, you can find fluorescent bulbs that produce a pleasant daylight spectrum and conveniently screw directly into incandescent fixtures.

SWITCHING TO COMPACT FLUORESCENTS

A 15w compact fluorescent bulb produces the same amount of light as a conventional 60w incandescent bulb. On top of that, these bulbs last many times longer, which more than compensates for their higher purchase price.

An easy way to save electricity is to add motion sensors to lights indoors and out. Just screw the sensor into the fixture and screw in the bulb. Because the light goes on only when there is activity—then turns off after a set amount of time—you can cut energy use by up to 90 percent. They are particularly useful for parts of the home that you typically visit only for a short period, such as hallways, bathrooms, closets, and the garage. They also turn on lights in places where your hands may be full, such as entryways and in storage spaces, the mudroom, and the laundry.

Fluorescent Lighting

Fluorescent bulbs used to give off a flickering, greenish light that made people look sick, though those days are past. They now come in full-spectrum hues that illuminate as naturally as halogen bulbs, and in their new compact form they screw into standard lamp sockets. Compact fluorescents cost more initially, but they use a quarter of the energy of incandescent bulbs and last 10 times longer. Keep in mind that these bulbs work best when left on for three minutes or longer; they are not the best choice for closets and hallways, where lights are used briefly and only occasionally.

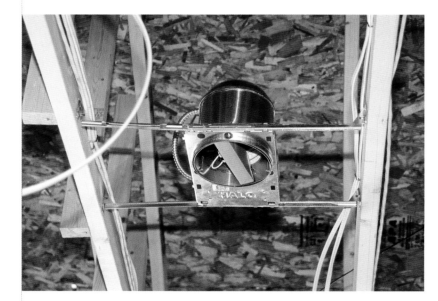

Recessed lights may look attractive, but consider the drawbacks. They are more expensive to retrofit than surface-mount fixtures, and they cast less light for a given wattage. Also, unless they're insulated and sealed, heat can escape.

Canned Light

Recessed can lights are built into soffits and ceilings during construction, and they may cost less to install than individual surface-mounted lights. They are particularly effective for directional or focal lighting, such as over a fireplace, the kitchen sink, or stair landings. But for a wall-washing effect—for example, to illuminate art—track lighting is quicker to put up and spreads light better than a recessed fixture.

History Meets Technology in Zero-Energy Remodel

Imagine a house so efficient that it allows the owner to make a profit selling energy back to the electric company.

That's the vision that inspired William Asdal of Asdal Builders in Chester, N.J. He owned a 1700s farmhouse by a very productive trout stream and had dreams of converting the property into a bed-and-breakfast. With the help of engineers from the U.S. Department of Energy and the National Association of Home Builders Research Center, he came up with a strategy that included a ground-source heat pump, a windmill for electricity, and photovoltaic panels for both electricity and hot water. As for conserving energy, the plan combined high levels of sealing and insulation. The result was the nation's first net zero-energy remodel.

Not until you go down into the basement is the advanced technology revealed. An orderly array of computers, PEX piping, voltage converters, and heat exchangers does the heavy work of turning wind, sun, and geothermal energy into heat, coolness, and electrical current.

From the outside, this historic house doesn't reveal the modern technological wizardry that provides light, heat, and cooling at no net cost.

Openings: Doors and Windows

EVERY DOOR IN A HOUSE IS AN INVITATION, every window an opportunity to expand and illuminate your indoor environment. This chapter explores ideas for creating openings that go beyond strictly functional. Of course doors should provide security, and windows are a key place for upgrading energy efficiency. Nonetheless, you've now come to a fun phase of remodeling, in which improvements yield aesthetic as well as practical benefits.

Like music and art, architecture can trigger emotions, through the manipulation of light and shadow and the suggestion of open space. Developers of expensive homes and apartments understand this, and their pitch is selling view, not walls. Windows and doors offer an opportunity to refresh and enliven every corner of your house, without expanding the footprint by a square foot.

By defining the front door with a new gabled porch and native flowering plants, the owners transformed an otherwise uninspired ranch into a very inviting home.

AFTER

Doors and windows used to be the biggest maintenance headaches a homeowner faced, because they were so vulnerable to the elements. But current models require virtually no upkeep. And new materials and tighter seals help lower fuel bills, which offsets the expense of buying and installing windows. Your project might even qualify for a tax break. That aside, buyer beware: You can easily spend a fortune on doors and windows without equal aesthetic or practical gains. Manufacturers often exaggerate the convenience and energy benefits of their products, when an hour with caulk and weather-stripping would serve just as well.

FRONT DOOR DECOR

Nothing transforms the image of a house as inexpensively and easily as remodeling the entry. You may not have the budget (or the architectural scale) to indulge in an impos-

ing portal and grand foyer. But by making the transition between the outside world and the intimacy of your abode more inviting, you can create a genuine emotional lift every time you—or anyone else—cross the threshold.

This is a matter of using a little discrimination, not spending lots of money. Instead of buying an expensive door, jazz it up with wider moldings, contrasting colors, and accent materials like tile. An entry says something about who lives inside, and the most interesting people I know care less about image than about imagination. Even if you're fairly traditional, the front door is one place where you can indulge in color and whimsy. And it's a tradition: Just tour London's mustiest stiff-lipped neighborhoods and you'll find front doors painted apple green, fire engine red, and lemon yellow. The front door can reveal a glimpse of the owner's inner life, with an implied invitation

BEFORE

Keep an eye out for modern building materials that combine durability, extraordinary energy efficiency, and good looks, such as insulated fiber-glass doors that accept stain almost like wood.

Even in the most staid neighbor-hoods of London, the front door always has a splash of color.

TO HAVE YOUR HOME MAKE A GOOD FIRST IMPRESSION, pay attention to the front door. It gives visitors a visual and tactile experience. Keep the door freshly painted in a diverting color, and splurge a bit on a high-quality handle.

Photo by: Sandi Witkowicz

The front door of a home can suggest a lot about the people who live inside.

and warning: If you don't like what you see, don't enter; but if you do like it, you'll feel right at home inside.

For instance, buy a plain, solid slab door and then use it like a canvas. For inspiration, go to the lumberyard and pick up a catalog of expensive entry doors. Then create an interesting pattern with applied moldings, ironwork, or objects you've collected. For example, place a birdhouse over the peephole on the front of the door, or combine a deadbolt with an iron gate pull in lieu of a doorknob.

You might allow the front door to take on a different look from the rest of your home. I have seen architects' houses set along old, tree-lined historical streets that have entries that are startlingly modernist—like the architect. Try taking an old frame-and-panel door and covering the raised sections with plastic laminate layered with a thin sheet of brass, copper, aluminum, or stainless steel. When given an acid-etched finish, the panels take on a patina that can be useful in making a comfortable transition between traditional and cutting-edge. And faux paint treatments can turn an ordinary door into an extraordinary statement. Applying a convincing faux finish requires some skill and an artistic touch, and local artisans can do the job if you aren't quite up to it.

Give some thought to protecting a handsomely painted door from the elements. A full-light storm door will shield the door while keeping it visible. You may prefer the look of a varnished exterior door, but unless you live in a very moderate climate, expect to have to deal with refinishing it every three to five years, unless it is protected by a storm door. Using a low-e finish will further protect a door from ultraviolet rays.

Replacement Doors

At some point, you may decide that a door is beyond help. New models with good insulation value and effective weatherstripping are available. Prehung units are particularly easy for amateur carpenters to install, but if yours is an older house, you may run into

AS YOU WEIGH THE DECISION ABOUT WHETHER TO REPLACE EXTERIOR DOORS, keep the potential energy savings in mind. New doors with a wood or fiberglass exterior and an insulated core can achieve levels of energy efficiency unmatchable with traditional frame-and-panel units.

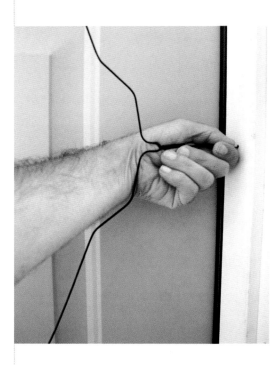

To measure the overall rough opening of a doorway, drill a small hole through the left- and right-hand jambs, insert a wire hanger into each hole until it makes contact with the rough frame, and then measure their depth. Add these two measurements to the width of the door to obtain the overall rough frame dimension. Do the same to measure the height of the rough opening.

TRADE SECRET STORM DOORS

If you decide to stick with an old door, you can improve its energy efficiency significantly with new weatherstripping, jamb insulation, and a storm door. The space between the storm door and entry door acts as a thermal barrier. Adding a storm door also protects the entry door from damaging ultraviolet rays, wind, and moisture. Storm doors have improved over the years, and you can now buy them with thermal glazing, tight weathersealing, and rugged hardware that will stand up to heavy use. In a sunny exposure, the heat trapped between the two doors can damage painted finishes. Make sure a new storm door provides some means of controlled ventilation.

out-of-square and odd-size rough openings. If you have an odd-size opening and buy a standard-size door, you risk turning the job into a major carpentry project. Instead, have somebody from your local a lumberyard measure the opening and custom-build a prehung unit.

To find out whether you can use an off-the-shelf unit or need a custom door, measure the rough opening this way: Drill a small hole through the jambs on either side of the opening and the header above until you reach the framing. Straighten the hook of a wire coat hanger and insert the wire into each of these holes until it hits the framing. Pull out the wire and measure how deep it went. Add these three measurements to that of the door width and height, and you'll have overall rough opening. You'll need to allow extra height, because modern prehung doors come with a threshold that makes them stand a bit taller than older ones. Once you've got the dimensions, see if manufacturers carry a standard size that will fit.

If you buy a new wood door, make sure to prime all six sides, including the top and bottom, before the wood has a chance to soak up moisture. The paint cracking you often see between a door's panels is typically caused by moisture wicking from the unseen (and unprotected) top and bottom surfaces.

I prefer a wood-grain fiberglass door to one made of wood. It can be finished with a solid-body stain, and if the result doesn't seem quite as handsome as the real thing now, it will hold up much better over the years. Fiberglass has a warmer look than steel doors, whose metal panels are susceptible to dents.

A Friendlier Facade

If you add an entry when remodeling, consider the home's architectural heritage. In this example, a somewhat severe foursquare house is given a more approachable look with an appropriately sized and detailed front porch.

FRONT ENTRANCE FACE-LIFT

A more ambitious approach to remodeling the entryway is to add a porch, portico, or even a narrow pediment. Like a new front door treatment, these projects can transform a nondescript address, although you may want to restrict yourself to changes that are somewhat in keeping with the architectural style of your house.

For ideas, consult an architectural field guide such as *The Visual Dictionary to American Architecture* (Owl Books, 1997) or, more to the point, *The Language of Doors* (Artisan, 2005). You can upgrade the entrance without it looking like an afterthought if you follow the outlines of period architecture. You'll also do well to follow the suggestions of an architect. Here is one way to proceed. Take a digital photo of your house, print it on plain paper, and ask an architect to overlay sketches of an appropriate design. This service won't cost a great deal, and it might save you from a big aesthetic mistake.

Entryway remodeling needn't be that expensive, because most of the construction is simply applied to the facade, like the nose and ears stuck onto a Mr. Potato Head®. You can snap on parts like a gable pediment, front stoop railings, portico benches, or a faux balcony over the front door. Add a new coat of paint and some new shingles, and you've changed the look of your home. You aren't upgrading so much as *detailing* a house that the builder didn't quite complete. If you think of your home's original construction as "stage one," then this is stage two, completing the original plan.

BEFORE

AFTER

Entrances, Plain and Not So

Even in period architecture, there was a range in design from cost-effective to more sophisticated and expensive. These versions of a Craftsman entrance show how you can detail the facade to suit your budget. The low concrete stoop and faux stone columns are as authentic and appropriate as the raised porch, railing, and square columns capped with elaborate detailing.

Simple

Straightforward detailing

Faux stone columns

Low concrete or wood porch

This otherwise unremarkable house is made charming with simple detailing at the entry, such as vinyl windows and siding, a steel-clad entry door, and plastic railing, all of it durable and needing little maintenance.

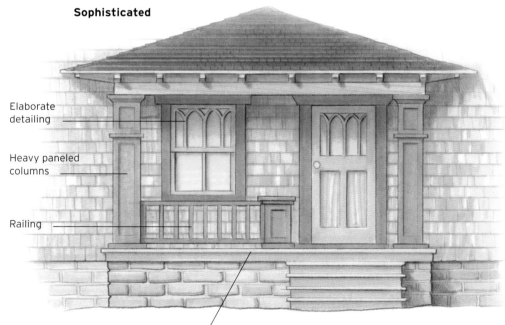

Sophisticated

Elaborate detailing

Heavy paneled columns

Railing

Full raised porch floor

We make these eaves brackets from treated 4x4s and 2x4s, paint them white, and install them with screws for an inexpensive Craftsman detail.

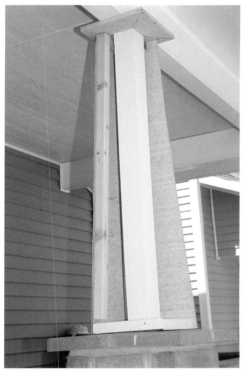

You can make tapered or square columns with a frame of 2x2s and exterior panel board cut to make the four equal sides. Or purchase two-piece prefabricated columns that fit around a structural (but visually spindly) 4x4.

By using baseboard instead of casing molding to trim a window or door, you create a deep, imposing frame at a lower cost than wide casing.

You can buy a remarkable range of prefabricated columns, brackets, Victorian moldings, and almost any historical filigree form. Even the installation of elaborate embellishments such as dentil moldings for a decorative frieze, volute capitals, pediments, and Greek Revival scrolls require little more than the ability to use a tape measure and a miter saw. Most of these moldings are available in composite plastics that accept paint without priming and will never rot.

Refashion the Reception Area

You don't really need a two-story foyer that's tall enough for a pet giraffe in order to receive guests in style. You can make a sensational statement by painting one wall in an accent color or using museum-quality recessed lighting to highlight a favorite painting. If your entry seems dull, allow natural light to add dramatic shadows and light; a full-light door, transoms, or sidelights are an opportunity to boost architectural interest without extensive remodeling. Add a large mirror to the entry, and you multiply the

Consistency can be costly and unnecessary. A small swatch of $75-per-yard carpet in the hallway makes an all but unnoticable transition to $20-per-yard carpet.

Before upgrading the front door, you may want to enliven an entry that sees more daily traffic—perhaps a mudroom, laundry room, or garage access. Make it comfortable, with a seating area for taking off shoes and boots.

IN COLDER CLIMATES, CHOOSE DOUBLE-PANE WINDOWS filled with argon gas for maximum R-value.

room's breadth and add the dynamic play of shifting light.

The foyer is usually small enough to provide an ideal backdrop for tightfisted extravagance. By using expensive items on a modest scale, you get maximum effect at minimum expense. In a small foyer, you can splurge on flooring, molding, ceiling details, and lighting without stressing your budget. It's a little way to make a big statement.

Even if your front door opens directly into your living room, you can define an entry with a shift in flooring materials, including tile, stone, and hardwood. The risk is that adding a small swatch of contrasting flooring can look awkward, as if you had stepped into a flooring showroom. To solve the problem of continuity, I like to bring the outside in. It makes visual sense to use the same material —slate or brick pavers, for example—for both the stoop and entry. To play up the effect and help the eye to make the connection, add a full-light door or sidelight. A simpler alternative is to establish the boundaries of the entry with an outline in a contrasting wood, tile insets, or even paint. Long-lasting floor paints are formulated to stand up to foot traffic, and they can be used to create subtle but highly customized accents. Cost: a gallon of paint and a roll of masking tape.

Another way to set off the front door from the living room is to add a low divider, with space for books or art objects on the living-room side and a low bench on the other. This creates just enough of a visual barrier for a sense of privacy when meeting someone in the foyer. Inexpensive wood columns can also define the entry without

closing it in. They stand sentry, defining the boundary between public space and the inner sanctum.

If the stairs are visible from the entry, you can upgrade the steps with wood treads or carpet them with a high-grade, textured-cut loop pattern such as diamonds, bows, pin dots, or fleurs-de-lis. These designs seem to "pop out" with a sculptural effect. Not only does a good carpet suggest expensive flooring throughout but it wears better on heavily used steps. I typically transition to a lower-grade carpet at the top of the stairs. If you choose your colors carefully and hire a good installer to seam the pieces, the switch between the two qualities will go unnoticed. In my own house, I used $75-per-yd. carpet on the steps, transitioning to $20-per-yd. carpet upstairs. My guests see only the nice stuff on the steps.

Other Entries, Other Options

In many homes, the front door is seldom used because most of the traffic enters through the mudroom, kitchen, or garage. I recommend remodeling this well-used area first, before tackling the showier parts of the house. The side or back door should be a well-organized spot, with coat hooks, a boot bench, an umbrella basket, and a sturdy place to set bags of groceries.

A subtle but important change is to use full-spectrum lighting to ease the transition between indoors and out. Place a piece of artwork or a vase with fresh-cut flowers where you'll spot it as you walk through the door. Add a mirror near the exit for a final grooming check on your way out.

If your door feels a little wobbly when shut and cold air blows in around the edges, consider replacing the door strike with a self-adusting Door-Tite™ lock strike (www. door-tite.com). This specialty strike is designed to replace the existing D-shaped strike. Six ridges on the tongue of the strike step back incrementally. Pushing the door closed causes the strike latch to engage and take up any troublesome slack.

BUY A RUN OF WROUGHT-IRON RAILING and bolt it outside of a second-floor slider to mimic a Mediterranean balcony.

A faux balcony railing of wrought iron makes visual sense of a second-story sliding door that was added to flood the master bedroom with light.

Use patio doors to take advantage of vistas—either grand or pocket-size—that otherwise would be unseen.

Wide-Open Spaces

So much of what we love about our homes lies beyond the four walls. As you plan a remodeling project, review ways of making the most of natural light, fresh air, long views, and easy access to the outdoors.

Patio doors double as both a picture window and as an entry. Sliding doors are the least expensive variation, and they come standard on many entry-level houses. But if you have a sliding door, chances are you may find yourself wanting to upgrade to a swinging door—one that doesn't bind, mislatch, or require a bodybuilder to operate. Because patio doors have so much glass, pay attention to the energy specifications. Always opt for dual-pane, low-e glazing.

If you want to enlarge the opening to take better advantage of a view and admit more light, go taller instead of wider. Manufacturers offer a range of door heights from the traditional 6 ft. 8 in. up to 8 ft. Taller doors look particularly elegant and require less carpentry to install than wider ones. Because the opening is already there, just remove the header and reinstall it at the adjusted height. If you install an 8-ft. door with no room for a header, take note of how the joists run. If they are parallel to the wall in which the patio door is set, you don't need a header. If they run perpendicular, you can usually rely on the band joist (along the edge of the room) to carry the load if you add joist hangers to the joists that rest over the door—but check with a building official, architect, or engineer.

Sliders don't work well in heavily trafficked areas. Still, there's no reason not to use them as big (but inexpensive) windows. To make sliding patio doors look more like windows, place them over a 12-in. curb wall. Or, use them at a second-floor landing to bring in loads of light, while screwing them fast so that they can't be operated. If you want to be able to open an above-grade slider for ventilation, install an exterior railing for safety.

In my remodeling projects, I like to install patio doors that open to a narrow side yard

This sliding unit from Andersen® installs easily into an existing opening. New sliders are an improvement over the doors you may have lived with, including steel rollers for smoother operation, natural wood interiors, and energy-efficient glazing.

rather than the backyard. This part of the property is typically a forgotten and unused space. I add an attractive feature (like window dressing, but in reverse) such as a trellis and landscape material, a wall fountain, or a small pond surrounded by flowering bushes. These miniscapes can be more eye-catching than a deep backyard, creating views that will enliven spaces within the home.

You can also use sliders *indoors* to close off rooms without cutting down on light. I like

to install them in the basement to set off an exercise room. They act as see-through walls that can be opened for added ventilation or closed to keep the sounds of a treadmill and disco tunes from disturbing everybody else. On the main floor, French-style units can bring in light—but not cold or unwelcome heat—from three-season porches or sunrooms. To open up an entire wall, it's possible to purchase multiple-slider units in widths up to 24 ft. But you get the same

Vinyl windows not only cost less but also deliver better energy efficiency and help deaden noises from outside. The hollow frame construction acts like the insulative gap between the panes in a dual-glazed window.

Photo by: Larry Douglas

An Arts and Crafts-style decal was placed over the window in a back door to block a less-than-attractive view and add a dash of color.

Photo by: Larry Douglas

Antique colored glass turns an ordinary basement window into an artistic statement.

effect for less money by simply coupling a row of standard off-the-shelf sliders.

WINDOW SHOPPING

Windows boost the mood indoors by bringing in fresh air and a quality of light that reveals the true colors of flooring, furniture, and art. They also allow the eye to wander beyond the confines of walls and ceilings. On the downside, windows account for about 50 percent of a typical home's heating and cooling loads. Highly efficient replacement units can improve that situation, with the added advantage of operating easily and tilting out for cleaning.

Vinyl replacement windows are usually the most cost-effective alternative and have the highest energy ratings. These windows also deaden exterior noise more effectively than wood or aluminum windows. They can be bought in any configuration: awning, casement, sliders, and single- and double-hung. Because of a vinyl window's superior thermal qualities, you can buy highly rated units with Energy Star certification for not much more than the cost of standard glazing.

You can order vinyl replacement windows that fit within the jambs of your existing sashes, for a window-within-a-window solution. This allows you to avoid reworking exterior and interior finishes. A disadvantage is that these windows have to be somewhat smaller, reducing the window area a bit. If your remodeling plans include adding new siding, you may want entirely new windows.

You can also simply buy replacement sash kits that fit into the existing jambs. This doesn't reduce the size of the opening as much as the window-within-a-window option, and replacement sashes are easy to install. They come with thin jamb liners that slip into the opening, but if the opening isn't perfectly square, the sashes may bind. That's why I prefer to avoid potential problems and completely replace old windows.

When you replace the sashes of an older window, make sure to insulate the large cavity that held the sash weights. Remove the window casing, fill the cavity with fiberglass

Window Lingo

When considering new windows for a remodeling, it's important to have a good window vocabulary.

Fixed

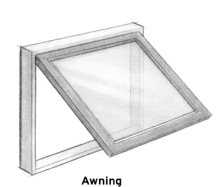

Awning

Casement

Pivot

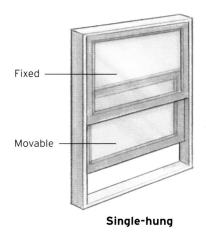

Fixed

Movable

Single-hung

Movable

Movable

Double-hung

This double slider fits in well because it has internal muntins that hark back to a traditional divided-light grid. Note the transom windows above.

Although jamb liners are less expensive, I prefer to replace an entire window because this assures me the whole assembly is energy efficient, not just the glazing.

CLEAR CHARACTER

Windows define the character of a building through their shape, size, construction, and arrangement on the facade. When you shop for windows as you remodel, give particular thought to the pattern of the muntins, on both the top and bottom sashes. Certain patterns are associated with particular architectural periods, although there is considerable overlap between one domestic style and another.

insulation or low-volume expanding foam, and reinstall the casing.

Sliders Are the Best Buy

Of the common window configurations, horizontal sliders cost the least, which should not suggest that they are cheap or inefficient. If latched tightly, they provide as good a seal as any window. And they look similar to casement windows that cost three and four times as much. Larger units can be heavy and difficult to open. So to create a large expanse of glass, flank a picture window with narrow sliders on either side. If you want to match the appearance of traditional double-hung windows elsewhere in the house, you can buy sliders with a muntin grid between the double panes.

Single-hung windows, with their one operable tilting sash, cost little if anything more than sliders, though an advantage of a double-hung unit is that you can open the upper sash a bit without creating desk-level gusts that blow your papers around the room. The extra ventilation also may be welcome in the kitchen and bathrooms, but take advantage of the lower cost of single-hung windows where you can.

Crank-operated casement windows work best where it would otherwise be difficult to open the window. For example, I recommend a casement window behind the kitchen sink. It's much harder to belly up to the counter and reach across to struggle with a double-hung or slider than it is to turn a crank. Casements also work best for a tall, narrow configuration. They provide a clear vertical view in a width that would be awkward for a slider.

Don't Guess on the Glazing

Listening to somebody who sells windows can make you feel like you've stepped into a computer store. Dual and low-e glazing, argon gas, tempered or laminated glass—the technology is apt to be confusing, but it pays to know what you're buying and why. No

If an existing window frame is in good repair, square, and level, installing jamb liners and new sashes is the least expensive replacement option.

A Matter of Muntins

Whether your windows have true divided lites or surface-applied simulated grills to mimic the old look, take care to choose replacements with the appropriate muntin pattern.

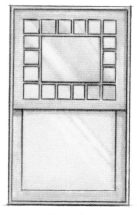

Prairie

Traditional

Two-lite

Top sash only

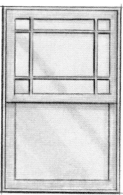

Victorian

ONE WAY TO SAVE MONEY WHEN REPLACING WINDOWS
is to analyze where you don't really need operable sashes. In
those spots, use a fixed pane instead.

With its easily turned
crank, a casement window
is the best choice for use
above the kitchen sink.

ECONOMICS OF REPLACEMENT WINDOWS

Bill Asdal of Asdal Builders in
Chester, N.J., came up with an
estimate of the payback period
for replacing aluminum windows
with low-e, double-glazed vinyl
windows, instead of with standard
double-glazed units. The coated
windows would add $400 in cost
but lower the annual fuel bill an
estimated $157, meaning that
the savings could be expected
to repay the investment in only
2½ years or so.

Initial cost	$3,528
Estimated annual saving	$157
Cost difference of upgrading to low-e instead of ordinary glazing	$400
Payback	2.5 years

one type of glazing is appropriate across the country, or on all four sides of your house for that matter. Learn the language of modern windows and maximize energy benefits while reducing costs.

First, a primer. Window performance improved dramatically after the energy crisis of the mid-1970s. Manufacturers began using multiple glazing layers to add air between panes as insulation. This helped with thermal transmission but added little more insulation than what you could get with a standard storm window. Adding inert gases, such as argon, improved the insulation further. Next, manufacturers began to coat windows with space-age films (yes, they were originally developed for NASA) that reflected UV radiation. These low-e coatings reflect heat back toward the source—on the outside, back to the sun, and on the inside, back into a warm room on cold winter nights. These coatings also help prevent sunlight from fading carpets, floors, and furniture.

Now think about the value of low-e glazing in climate like Arizona's. Pretend you have large picture windows across the back of your house, which faces due west. As the afternoon progresses, your house gets very hot. Windows with low-transmission, low-e coatings would help immensely. Now imagine the north side, where the few windows you have are shaded by some trees. Here you do without the expense of low-e glazing, at no notable loss in energy efficiency.

When replacing your windows, consider the orientation of your house and buy low-e glazing only where it will reduce solar gain. Another point to keep in mind is that there

Interior solar shades keep out heat while providing an unobstructed view. The fabric diffuses light and blocks ultraviolet rays, keeping rooms cool and preventing furniture from fading.

are different types of this high-performance glass, for different applications.

In a mixed climate with cold winters and hot summers, it pays to use *selective* low-e coatings that reflect most, but not all, of the heat gain from the sun. In cold climates, you want as much solar gain as possible while you minimize winter heat loss, so a *high-transmission* coating works best.

Solar Screens

Fiberglass window screens can do more than keep bugs at bay. Solar versions block varying percentages of solar radiation, as appropriate for your climate. Because they

DON'T INSTALL A SEALED STORM WINDOW OVER LEADED GLAZING on a sunny side of the house, or the resulting high temperatures may melt the lead.

STORM WINDOWS

Single-glazed windows with storm sashes have steadily lost market share to double-pane units. Yet storms still have a place on older homes, where the traditional look of the sashes is to be preserved. They also will serve well enough if your budget doesn't allow replacing the existing windows with modern thermal units. And you might look into buying storm windows with low-e glazing for better performance. Although a big drawback of traditional storm windows is that they are a hassle to put up, take down, and clean, you can order storm windows that mount on the *inside* of the opening, a boon where outside access to the windows is difficult and where historical preservation codes prohibit standard storms.

These low-e storm windows provide significant energy savings and also fit the character of the home, located in a historical neighborhood.

can significantly reduce the air-conditioning, load some utilities subsidize their installation. Like low-e glazing, these screens work best on east- and west-facing exposures, where the relatively low sun slips below awnings, trellises, and roof overhangs. To further moderate the force of the sun, install shades made from UV-blocking textiles. Unlike permanent screens, these can be rolled quickly to take full advantage of the view.

Upgrading Historical Treasures

You may prefer to keep the original windows if they have historical and aesthetic value. It's possible to improve their energy efficiency by installing storm windows or directly

applying tinted, reflective, and low-e films to the glass. These films moderate solar heat gain, reduce furniture-fading UV rays, and even add an attractive tint to the incoming light—a little like church windows. With less unwanted heat pouring in, it may be possible to reduce the size of the air-conditioning equipment you'd planned for the remodel.

Rx for Wounded Windows

Rotted and damaged window frames may appear beyond hope, but various epoxy products can give them new life. Epoxy *consolidators* are brushed or poured on to stabilize and strengthen decayed wood; a puttylike epoxy is then used to build up

This magical space was created by installing three ordinary double-hung windows in a cantilevered bay.

missing wood. Once cured, the filler can be cut, sanded, and painted like wood. Repaired areas are strong enough to accept hardware, and unlike other wood fillers, epoxy will not shrink or fail over time.

SUNNY SPOTS

A bay window will improve views and bathe the room in light and warmth, which is why adding a bay is one of the most popular remodeling projects, even though it's not inexpensive. You can create the same effect for less money by assembling standard windows in a half-hexagon pattern. If the bay is supported by cantilevered joists and extends

INSIDE LOOKING OUT

Pretend the view outside your window is a landscape painting, and then turn your attention to framing it properly, as an artist might. You can emphasize the impression of distance by deepening the molding around the window—although as a rule of thumb, the better the view, the less you require in the way of a frame.

Window Seats

You can create a window nook even in a conventional straight-walled room by building in storage units on either side of a set of two or three windows.

An ordinary window can be made special by building a window seat and thickening the adjacent walls.

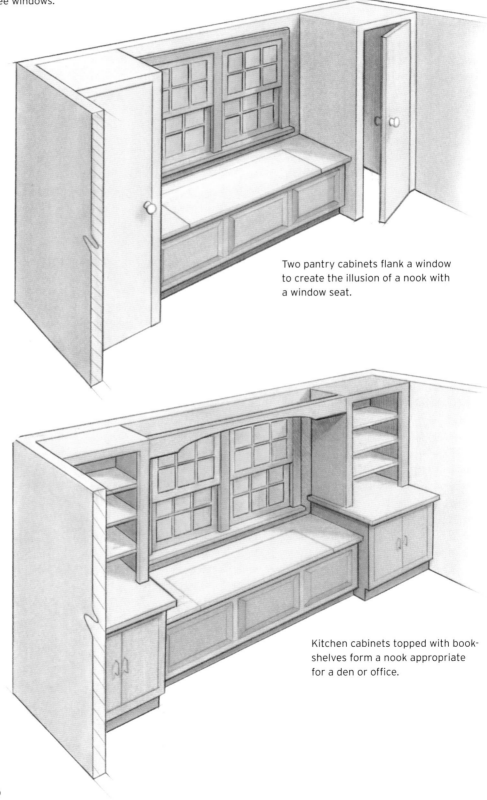

Two pantry cabinets flank a window to create the illusion of a nook with a window seat.

Kitchen cabinets topped with book-shelves form a nook appropriate for a den or office.

This corner resembles a bay window, but it's not. You can re-create a similar seating area using double-hung windows, a plywood box for the seat, and custom cushions ordered from an upholstery shop.

With their 180-degree view, bay windows create a scene that can lift the spirit.

no more than 2 ft., you won't need an added foundation.

By setting two or more windows adjacent to each other in a corner, you can get the light and broad views of a bay window without the cost. These transparent corners are appealing sites for sunny breakfast nooks, and potted plants do especially well in them.

You can create the effect of a bay window by extending the room's surfaces *into* the room. Build out the interior walls all around a window with bookshelves or simply with studs and drywall, and add a window seat.

SPECIALTY WINDOWS

You can find all sorts of inexpensive, quirky windows that—in the right place—add architectural interest to your house. My

Aiming a Skylight

By shifting the lightwell to one side or the other, you can direct its lighting effect to your best advantage. Consider leaving the rafters exposed for a striking (if necessary) architectural feature.

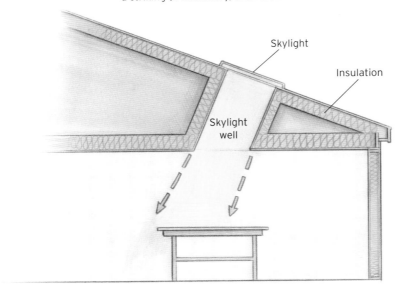

Skylight

Insulation

Skylight well

A Splayed Skylight

By framing a splayed lightwell that widens toward the bottom, you can increase the illumination from a small skylight in the same way that a megaphone amplifies sound.

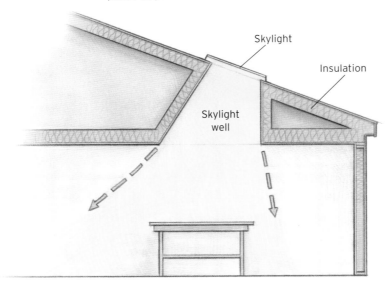

Skylight

Insulation

Skylight well

favorites include windows under kitchen cabinets, square windows tilted 45 degrees for a diamond shape, glass block inserts, and specialty glazing, such as glue-chip, beveled, and textured glass.

Skylights

Skylights perform the neat trick of bringing daylight into the darkest interior spaces of the home. This is especially valuable in small areas like bathrooms and hallways that otherwise would feel confining. Adding a skylight requires cutting rafters and ceiling joists and framing a lightwell. You can simplify the process by using a smaller skylight that fits between a pair of rafters, then

A skylight with splayed sides can transform a room with plenty of daylight and added headroom.

This interior window with backlighting brings a sense of connection with the outdoors to an otherwise windowless basement.

Sandblasted acrylic inserts lend a lantern-like luminosity to this inexpensive railing.

framing a funnel-shaped shaft that widens as it descends. If a ceiling joist or two are left exposed, use them to mount lighting. To make the joists look like an intentional feature, clad them with drywall.

Skylights have advantages that standard windows do not. In a bathroom, a skylight affords a discreet way to let in the sun and stars without offering a view to passersby. In a dark kitchen, a skylight brings in daylight without sacrificing wall space for cabinets.

A Solatube® lets you deliver light from the rooftop to a bottom story. This is a small, roof-mounted skylight attached to a reflective tube. Cut a hole in the roof, angle the tube to reach the desired location, and cut a hole in the ceiling. Lights in the tube illuminate the room at night as well.

Windows Within

Windows aren't just for exterior walls. As you plot your remodeling, look for ways of working windows into solid walls to help define rooms while allowing views. Placed at the end of a hallway or in a basement, an interior window can bring in daylight (or artificial light that will seem like the real thing) to brighten an otherwise somber space.

Visit a high-end loft apartment, and you will see ways in which architects and designers used translucent screens to make a tight space feel spacious. Japanese rice paper

Old sashes can serve a second life as see-through room dividers. You'll find racks full of single-glazed divided-light windows at most architectural salvage stores. But keep in mind that the glass is not tempered, making it unsafe for installation near doorways or lower than 18 in. from the floor.

Using either rigid or flexible ducting extensions, a tubular skylight connects to a diffuser in the ceiling. Although it does not provide as much illumination as a standard skylight, installation is easier, and you can direct a circle of light sufficient to illuminate a closet, laundry room, or hallway.

screens are a traditional approach, but you can use sheets of inexpensive acrylic in the same way. These modern plastics come in various finishes, from clear to elaborately textured. A milky white acrylic panel, softly illuminated from behind, will simulate daylight in a room without a window.

Use these panels in the basement, and it will no longer seem to be underground. Frame a basement window with an oversize window casing and replace the glazing with translucent acrylic. Paint the wall behind the window a reflective color that bounces light so that the pane will glow—at a lot less expense than adding a window well.

Transparent block is an attractive way to admit light and also maintain privacy. It can serve this purpose in bathrooms or on any wall that faces public areas. Glass block is pricey to install, but new acrylic units don't require a mason. This lightweight block installs like windows and comes with a nailing flange. Their prismatic effect casts light deep into a room for better illumination.

At the end of the hallway, two museum-quality fluorescent lights set the artwork aglow.

Architecturally Sensitive Storms

An older home can be made more energy efficient in ways that don't compromise its appearance. While remodeling their house in Lincoln, Neb., the Martin family had insulation blown into the walls. And instead of tearing out the leaky old windows with their leaded glass, they tracked down a company that would build black storm window frames, dual glazed and with a low-e coating. The architecture remains unblemished, and the home is toasty in winter and cool in summer without exorbitant utility bills.

This original porch swing hangs in the original porch at Martin family's historically restored house in Lincoln, Neb. Instead of replacing the original glazing, the Martins chose to preserve the old sashes behind high-quality, architecturally appropriate storm windows.

6

The Interior Canvas

WHEN REMODELING A ROOM, imagine you're working with six canvases: four walls, a floor, and a ceiling. Remodeling is your opportunity to transform these surfaces into the perfect background for entertaining your friends, relaxing with family, or sitting alone in calm contemplation. In this chapter, I'll offer ideas for creating an environment that sustains your interests and expresses your lifestyle.

IMPROVEMENT STARTS AT THE TOP

Builders typically make ceilings white, flat, and boring, which gives you plenty of room for improvement. "Ceiling white" is not a particularly natural hue; by adding another tint, you can start to redefine a room. As for the flatness, consider that a ceiling gives you more

Faux paint above the mantel extends the color and impact of the slate below for a towering effect, without tiling the whole wall. The high ceiling works well in the social environment of the room.

The abstract pattern on the ceiling was created with nothing but the most ubiquitous builders' medium, drywall.

architectural freedom than walls and floors because you don't have to worry about colliding with whatever embellishment you add to it. You can drop, raise, and punctuate this often-overlooked surface, treating it as a three-dimensional sculpture.

Break It Up

You've probably noticed that a low ceiling tends to suggest privacy and protection, characteristics that are conducive to intimate conversation, while a high ceiling signals a more public area. That's why a dramatically vaulted ceiling makes more sense in a living room than in a breakfast nook. Your remodeling plans might include lowering a ceiling to define a cozy corner or two.

It's more challenging to raise a ceiling in a room you want to make feel more important or formal, but it's not impossible. In a single-story house, you could claim a portion of the attic, as described in chapter 3 (see "Raising

LIGHT-COLORED CEILINGS DRAW THE EYE UPWARD and create a sense of height, while dark ceilings tend to keep the focus on the room's walls, furnishings, and accessories.

Raising the Roof

If you're able to replace the roof on a room, there's no need to settle for a flat ceiling. New roof trusses make it possible to transform a room with a dramatically vaulted ceiling.

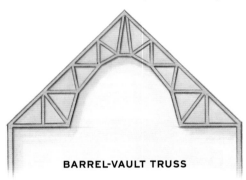

BARREL-VAULT TRUSS

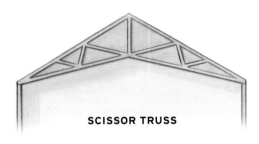

SCISSOR TRUSS

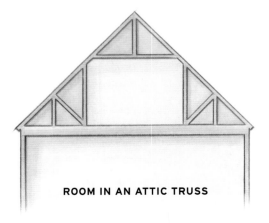

ROOM IN AN ATTIC TRUSS

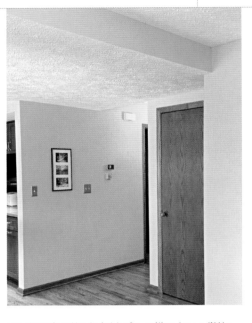

By changing the height of a ceiling by as little as 12 in., you can define a room as a special place. You can raise or lower the ceiling in the room itself, or do so in adjoining spaces for the same effect.

the Ceiling," p. 74). You could also reframe the roof with roof trusses designed to open up the space above the ceiling. Commercially available trusses can create interior vaults, coffers, and even domes.

The structure of your house or your budget may preclude such grand gestures. But you can still give your living room a lift by the careful use of "optical illusions." If you lower the perimeter of the living room with a soffit, the central part of the room will feel taller. Add to the effect by lowering the ceiling of the adjacent hallway, even if by only 6 in.; when you or your guests walk from the hall into the living area, the added perception of greater headroom will contribute an emotional lift. Or instead of lowering

This arched ceiling, set within a dropped soffit, combines a light trough and faux paint finish to dramatically set off a dining area.

Leftover bamboo flooring serves as a decorative ceiling treatment in this hallway. Pictures on the wall are indirectly illuminated by daylight-spectrum bulbs concealed behind the lowered ceiling.

A lowered ceiling can create a cozy nook and serve to emphasize the height of surrounding rooms.

the ceiling in the hall, make it lower by paneling it.

Color works in a similar way. Dark colors lower the apparent level of a ceiling, while light colors raise it. Play with slightly different shades to create subtle modulations between rooms. For example, paint the hallway ceiling with the full-strength hue. Then ask the paint store to cut the tinting formula in half for the adjacent room. Although the difference can be so subtle that no one comments, the effect is quietly remarkable. Remember that not every detail in your house needs to advertise itself; quiet touches can make a big difference in how an environment is experienced.

A SOFFIT UPLIFT

Creating a ceiling soffit involves building a drywall box. If you incorporate a lighting cove within the soffit, you can wash the raised portion of the ceiling with light, visually lifting it further. This effect is not limited to whole rooms; you can create the same illusion in the recessed area of the ceiling over a dining table or over the bed in a master bedroom. This is especially effective in defining a center of activity within a large room.

A Glow from Above

A ceiling can be lowered a few inches to hide banks of fluorescent fixtures, which then cast their diffuse light along the walls.

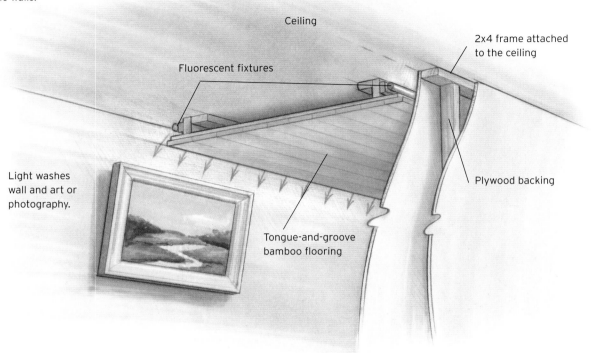

Ceiling

Fluorescent fixtures

2x4 frame attached to the ceiling

Plywood backing

Light washes wall and art or photography.

Tongue-and-groove bamboo flooring

Highest Distinctions

Use inexpensive moldings to create the egg-crate pattern of the richly detailed coffered ceilings found in formal and Craftsman rooms. Have a look at the variety of MDF (medium-density fiberboard) moldings available at your home center. MDF is manufactured from wood fibers and synthetic resin, and it has a texture that's more consistent than wood and less prone to splitting, expanding, and contracting. It's also less expensive. If you want more detail, add layers of simple molding, such as a 1x4 capped by a 1x2. Keep in mind that any molding with routed detail will require greater skill to install, because the joints have to be *coped*—more of a challenge than simply butting up square cuts.

To see if the coffered look will work, measure the outline of your room. Should you divide it into thirds, fourths, or fifths?

Do you want to have the lines converge on a central figure, such as a diamond shape? How do the proportions work relative to the size of the space? Once you've arrived at a design, lay out the pattern on graph paper and make adjustments as necessary.

To make sure the job goes smoothly, create a full-size practice pattern. Cover the floor with resin-impregnated paper or kraft paper. Draw the ceiling pattern on it with chalk or a marker. Occasionally, look up at the ceiling for an idea of how the moldings will look. When you're satisfied with the layout, transfer the pattern to the ceiling. Locate the ceiling joists with a stud finder, and attach the pieces of molding with finishing nails and construction adhesive.

To add to the impression of depth, play up the contrast between the moldings and the ceiling. Paint the squares of ceiling between the moldings with a light, flat shade

PRO TIP

Produce an elegant coffered ceiling very simply, using a frame of 1x4s along with a two-tone paint scheme.

Courtesy of Lolita Dirks

A Coffered Effect

The egg-crate look of a coffered ceiling can be suggested with contrasting paint hues and a simple grid of lumber.

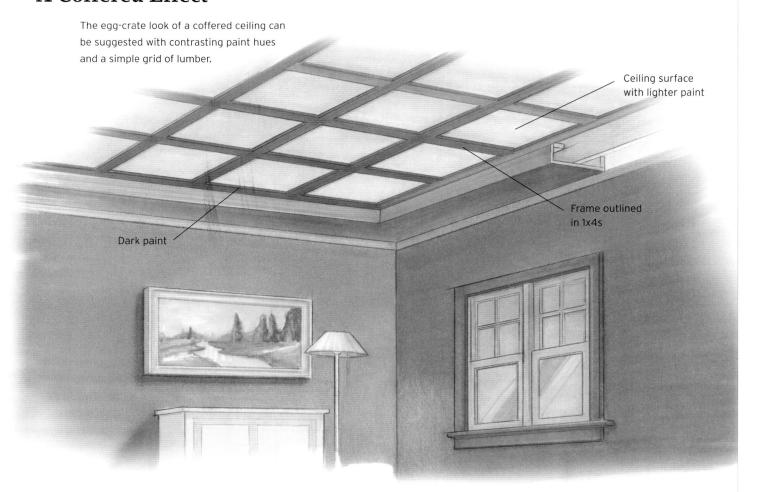

Ceiling surface with lighter paint

Frame outlined in 1x4s

Dark paint

Photo courtesy of Fifth Wall Designs

This coffered ceiling installs easily on rails suspended from the ceiling, making it possible to conceal new ductwork, plumbing, and electrical lines. The job goes quickly, even if the ceiling above is defective.

TRADE SECRET
ADDING TO SUBTRACT

If you are confronted with a structural beam that visually cuts a room in half, a novel remedy is to install a parallel series of false beams, spaced so that the real one seems to fit right in.

The line of ceiling paint that scribes the wall in this room serves two purposes. It simulates a crown molding and plays down the beam that would otherwise separate the room into two awkward rectangles.

Paneled Soffit

For an attractive soffit, install a row of the small doors intended for cabinets above a refrigerator. Use either flat panel doors or spend somewhat more for the raised-panel style. Run 1-by trim between the doors and along the top and bottom edges. Caulk the joints and paint with enamel.

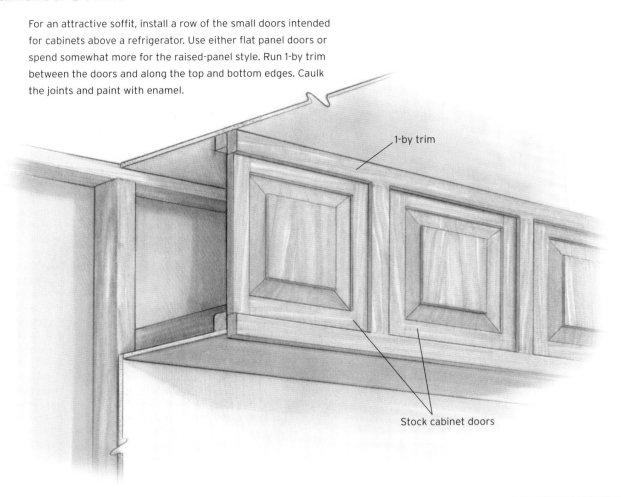

1-by trim

Stock cabinet doors

and the moldings themselves with darker, high-gloss enamel.

For a more detailed and especially elegant coffered ceiling, create a pattern that allows you to panel the ceiling with stock frame-and-panel cabinet doors. You can paint them or finish them clear. This isn't an inexpensive treatment, but it will cost far less than having a skilled artisan produce an authentic coffered ceiling. And you can make the project still more affordable by applying the panels to only a small area, such as over the dining-room table. A row of cabinet doors can also be attached along the edge of a soffit for the look of custom millwork.

If you want the real thing—a wood-paneled coffered ceiling—you can buy a moderately priced drop-ceiling kit that

includes hardwood rails and panel inserts. The rails are suspended from the ceiling with wires on toggle bolts. This approach is especially cost effective if you have an old, uneven plaster ceiling, because you are spared the repairs. After the grid rails are up, drop the panels in place. The hollow between the new ceiling and old makes it easy to add recessed lighting or to hide new ductwork.

A Crowning Achievement

An ample crown molding can make a room look elegant, though for a price. Traditional built-up molding requires layers of different trim profiles, precisely coped at the corners. A less expensive alternative is to layer drywall, vinyl crown molding, and the L-bead strips used to form drywall corners. You can

Crown molding runs well above the normal line of sight, and yet it goes a long way toward completing the look of a room. Installing this molding is more of a challenge than those that lie flat on the wall because of the involved corner cuts.

Drywall Molding

You can use layering techniques to build a custom crown molding out of drywall. The Trim-Tex drywall components illustrated here are available through drywall supply stores. Finish with drywall compound, then sand and paint.

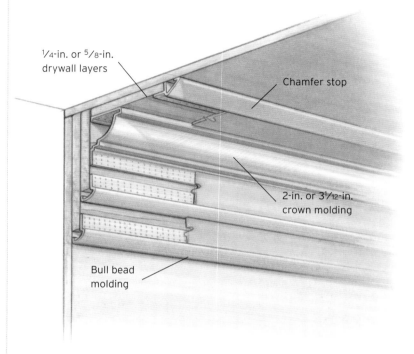

¼-in. or ⅝-in. drywall layers

Chamfer stop

2-in. or 3½₁₂-in. crown molding

Bull bead molding

The crown molding in this room was made from two pieces of inexpensive flat trim, one on the wall and the other running parallel along the ceiling. When painted the same color as the trim elsewhere in the room, the result looks impressive.

assemble this version of a crown molding with little but a drywall knife, scissors, and drywall compound.

In a room with a tall ceiling, you can use sleight of hand to create the effect of crown molding without the labor or expense. Simply place two parallel strips of narrow decorative molding around the room. Set one along the wall about 6 in. below the ceiling, and the other on the ceiling about 8 in. out from the wall. Apply satin trim paint to the decorative moldings as well as to the wall and ceiling areas between them to suggest the look of one large, built-up crown molding.

A variation on this project is to install molding 8 in. to 16 in. below the ceiling,

then paint both the ceiling and the walls above the molding a different color from the rest of the room. This will make the ceiling appear taller, and it works especially well in an old house with an uneven ceiling line because the eye will note the band of color instead.

Delicate Deceptions

In a room with a tall ceiling where the crown molding remains well above eye level, a slight deception can reproduce the effect of expensive wide crown molding. Simply draw a line on the wall around the room about 6 in. below the ceiling and draw another line on the ceiling at about 8 in. off the wall. After installing these two parallel lines

around the room, apply two coats of satin trim paint inside the lines, covering the molding, and the ceiling and wall between the moldings, with one solid band of color. The appearance will be that of a wide and elegant crown molding

You can achieve a similarly elegant effect by scribing the room with a single molding, such as a 1x4 placed 8 in. to 16 in. below the ceiling, and then paint the ceiling and top portion of the wall and trim the same color. This make the ceiling appear taller. The technique works especially well in an old house that has an uneven ceiling line. If you install your molding perfectly level, the uneven line of the ceiling disappears once everything is painted.

Reclaimed baseboard was used as a crown molding to hide the unevenness of a 150-year-old ceiling while accenting the room's formal appearance.

EMBOSSED WALLPAPER CAN CAPTURE THE DETAILS of a traditional tin ceiling; and, once painted, it looks convincingly similar to metal.

AFTER

BEFORE

When Lisa and Mat Inness readied their 1800s house to receive paying guests for afternoon tea, they replaced the unattractive tiled ceiling (below) with Armstrong tiles embossed to appear like a tin ceiling. With a coat of gilded paint, the effect is strikingly elegant.

Laminate plank flooring was used on the ceiling of this sunroom to suggest an informal atmosphere. The planks aren't of a very durable grade, but they're in no danger of wearing out in their present location.

These hollow columns look like stone but are made of lightweight, high-density foam board. You can find everything from ceiling medallions to Roman columns in foam. These products mimic plaster, stone, and rough-hewn wood, and install easily with adhesives.

Eclectic Ceiling Treatments

By thinking of the ceiling as a counterpart to the floor, you can free yourself to imagine using all kinds of materials that will keep you looking up. Armstrong® has reintroduced the classic acoustic ceiling tile—so widely used for basement ceilings—but with a twist. You now can buy tiles that look like tin panels, with stamped patterns that are difficult to distinguish from the real thing once you paint them with a metallic finish.

Lightweight plastic laminate flooring works well on ceilings for inexpensive accents and textures. Apply it with contact cement. For the look of a vacation lodge, you might use wood laminate plank flooring. Or, consider using bead-board-patterned plywood with its traditional appearance. You can even create the look of a mosaic-tiled ceiling by using vinyl floor tile. This might sound odd, but as an accent within the frame of a coffered ceiling, the effect can be stunning.

Beamed Ceilings

Lightweight, faux wood beams can add a rustic touch to a kitchen, living room, or den.

They can bring the level of an overtall ceiling (the kind you're likely to find in many houses built during the 1890s) down to a more human scale while adding warmth and an engaging relief. Styrofoam® moldings and ceiling beams are less durable (but how durable do they need to be attached to the ceiling?) but cut easily with a knife, stain like wood, and go up with glue. You can also make false ceiling beams by building a three-sided box out of 1x lumber. A company called Virtual Timbers® produces three-sided beams from real wood. Made of Douglas fir, these beams look authentic, even up close, and can be textured and stained just like solid timbers.

LIGHTEN UP

Next to paint, lighting may be the easiest way to change the appearance of an interior. Consider that dining in a romantic restaurant, having a fireside conversation, and watching a dramatic sunset are all events shaped by light.

To regulate lighting without changing fixtures, add dimmer switches in bedrooms

WHEN PLANNING THE LIGHTING OF YOUR HOME, THINK LIKE A PHOTOGRAPHER. Use light not only to see but also to illuminate objects (and people) in the best possible way.

Photo by: Roe Osborn

Some fixtures cast sculptural effects of shadow and light that add an architectural effect.

and living areas. If you have old dimmers, you may benefit by replacing them with new, energy-efficient models. Stay away from bottom-of-the-line dimmers, which tend to cause incandescent bulbs to buzz annoyingly.

A dimmer may not provide you with enough of an illumination range for a room that sees a number of activities. If you use your dining room for eating, paying bills, and reading the paper, you want a variety of options, from candlelight to task lighting.

That calls for *layered lighting,* with multiple light sources. The dining room might combine a central chandelier for mealtimes with several recessed lights for reading and paperwork. All should be on dimmers to allow you to tailor the light level.

Cheap Chandeliers

Chandeliers aren't just for dining rooms anymore. Use a pair of miniature chandeliers as nightstand lighting. To add character to

You can use inexpensive light fixtures tucked into architectural details to both illuminate and highlight the interesting features of your house.

Photo by: David Duncan Livingston

Track lighting has gone upscale, with attachments that range from traditional spots to elegant pendants. The flexibility of these systems allows you to fine-tune the location of lighting in playing up both architectural features and artwork.

TO ACCENT THE ART ON YOUR WALLS FOR A GALLERY LOOK, run track lights with small halogens around the room, placing them about 2 ft. out from the walls. Then paint the rectangle defined within the tracks with a different shade than the perimeter of the ceiling.

PRO TIP

PRO TIP

THE BARE-BULB HOLLYWOOD STYLE OF VANITY LIGHT STRIPS CREATES A GLARE. Instead, use pendants or mini chandeliers above the mirror or to the right and left of the mirror to make it easier to apply makeup or shave.

Using a Tigerbox®, that holds the box in place without nailing, you can easily retrofit a lighting junction box in the wall without having to do any patching.

Chandeliers are something of a bold departure from the recessed lights you'd expect to see in a kitchen, and they can provide excellent illumination as well.

a hallway, line it with three or more 16-in. chandeliers instead of flush ceiling lights, which are the unimaginative standard. Chandeliers don't cost less than cheap hall lights, but they have a higher pizzazz-per-dollar factor.

Another way of achieving the same thing at lower cost can be created with track lighting. Using a bendable-rail lighting system of flexible track, you can turn a whimsical spiral or S-shape by hand to accommodate the size and shape of the lighting area—and simultaneously complement the decor. Track lights now come with sophisticated accessories, including prim-to-playful pendants that work well in almost any setting. In fact, you could buy more than one set of pendants and change the mood according to the occasion: a chandelier for Thanksgiving dinner, and bar pendants for a cocktail party.

Showy Sconces

Wall lights have become a popular option in foyers, stairways, and dining areas. You can save when installing these lights by pulling power off a wall socket and running a switch within the same wall cavity; that saves you the expense of snaking wires up into the

Wall lights typically cost less to retrofit because you can run power to them from a wall socket more easily than you could to a ceiling fixture. You might also consider installing a wireless switch.

The creative use of dry-wall adds textural variety to what would have been a plain, conventional wall.

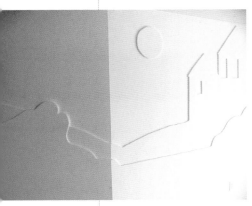

ceiling. Some sconces cast interesting, even sculptural patterns of light on the wall—an effect that can take the place of hanging artwork.

Indirect Lighting

Indirect lighting affords a miserly means to create drama. When the light source is hidden, there's no need to splurge on the fixture. A good-quality fluorescent shop light or even a plain porcelain lamp holder will do. All you need to ensure good lighting is a good bulb. Indirect lighting behind ceiling soffits creates a soft effect. Lights placed behind a mirror or wall hanging will make these objects more of a focal point. Rope lighting or fluorescent fixtures installed in a built-up trough around the edge of a floor will seem to buoy up the floor as if suspended. Nowadays you can even buy a flexible, drywall channel that accepts LCD rope lighting for creating interesting shadows and accents–such as floor lighting integrated into the baseboard.

Swanky Switches

Something basic and plain that presents the opportunity for expressing your creativity is the light switch in your guest bath or powder room. This presents an excellent occasion to make a subtle, but significant impression. Although a decorative switch can cost 10 times as much as an ordinary one, the total dollar amount remains small. Still, to save while splurging on switches, use the decorative ones only in the public places likely to receive notice, then use the ordinary, toggle switches everywhere else.

You can also use fancy switch covers, such as the stainless steel covers used in industrial settings, to make a subtle, but noticeable statement. In my office, I had the electrician install the sensual switches, but instead of following through with the matching (and very pricey) outlet covers, I used ordinary three-prong outlet plates. Nobody has ever noticed the outlets, but almost everyone who walks into the lavatory exits saying, "Neat switches." After that, they notice the cool switches throughout the office. It was a tiny upgrade with enough clout to provoke conversation; and came with a cost that, well, wasn't enough for me even to remember.

CREATIVE WALLS

It's impossible to overemphasize the value of paint in remodeling affordably. As I sit here writing in my home office, I can look up at a wall I've painted a deep, plummy red, and it makes me happy. One wall is all it takes to set this room apart as my special place. And contrary to popular opinion, deep colors don't reduce the perceived size of a room. They expand it, creating a vanishing point some distance away. Light colors make a room feel *brighter*, but not bigger.

If a room seems small and pinched, add depth by painting the back wall a darker color. Or extend its visual dimension into an adjoining space by carrying a wall finish across the two rooms. Conversely, you can delineate an area that feels overexposed, such as a dining room off a large living room, by using molding, a shift in color, or an applied texture, just as a picture frame sets off the world within a painting.

Another way to add depth is to paint one wall a slightly different shade of the room color. Ask the paint store to prepare 2 gal. of paint with only half the pigment in one can. Apply the full-strength paint to the surface you want to seem distant; on the rest of the room, use the lighter shade. The effect is subtle enough that you will be the only

A coat of just the right hue of paint can add panache without much cash. It's the contrast between the walls and white trim that make this room more than a 10-ft. by 10-ft. box.

The simplest and least expensive means of transforming an environment comes with color. Although we can all paint, it pays to learn the steps to proper prep and execution so people are surprised when you say, "I did it myself" (instead, they're thinking, "yeah, I can tell").

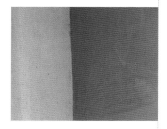

Photo by: Addison Doty

Clay plasters are more expensive than paint, but they can relieve walls of the sameness that afflicts homes with room after room of painted drywall. This finishing technique has the unusual effect of making interiors feel warmer in winter and cooler in summer.

This fireplace was constructed inexpensively, with a thin coat of exterior plaster over the framed drywall relief that hovers over the firebox. The drywall wave adds a bit of whimsy.

one who knows just how you expanded the sense of added space.

You can exploit color for a sense of comfort, too. In a warm climate, you might refresh the home with jewel tones, touches of coral and jade, and cool colors. Deeper shades can help thaw you out in a wintry climate; consider how you'd feel surrounded by walls of warm cinnamon, auburn, or burnt orange.

To help ensure that your house doesn't become a rainbow-colored mess, start with a neutral or anchor color that carries throughout the house. It should be an agreeable shade that harmonizes with your furniture and your home's dominant flooring. This color will be the background for any dramatic accents you choose to add. Good candidates for highlighting include the architectural elements that distinguish your home, such as a stairway, fireplace, or nook.

Originally designed as deck railing, EZ Rail™ can be used on short flights of stairs to accommodate any pitch. Simply align the bottom rail parallel with the existing stair, trim to fit, and screw in place.

Plain drywall tends to have a sterile look because of its lack of texture. An unusual remedy is to finish the walls with a refined form of mud instead of paint. Commercially available clay plasters are typically mixed with water, then troweled on in two coats to create mottled coloring and interesting textural variations. The resulting wall can become the dominant feature of a room.

Drywall Trim

Drywall is one of the cheapest building materials, which may be why its possibilities are usually overlooked. You can use it to create wainscoting, picture frames, art alcoves, easy arches, and even moldings around windows and doors. Recently introduced drywall products allow you to build inexpensive DIY-friendly crown moldings, baseboards, and chair rails. Lest you think decorating with drywall is a cut-rate alternative, consider that plaster—not wood—was traditionally

Coupled with color, drywall can even be layered into a three-dimensional mural.

No fancy cutting is required with EZ Rail balusters, which pivot as needed within the stair railing channel.

TURNING A CORNER WITH DRYWALL

Drywall bead is run along corners where two surfaces meet. That's simple enough, but bead is now available in a number of materials and configurations. You have a choice among metal, vinyl, paper-covered metal, and paper-covered plastic, in straight form or rolls. There are bullnose beads of 3/8 in. to 1 1/2 in., each of which is available in different profiles. You'll find beads available for off-angles, both inside and outside. There even are beads notched in order to run fiber optics.

Niche with a Lip

A niche between studs can be fitted with a simple ledge to provide more depth.

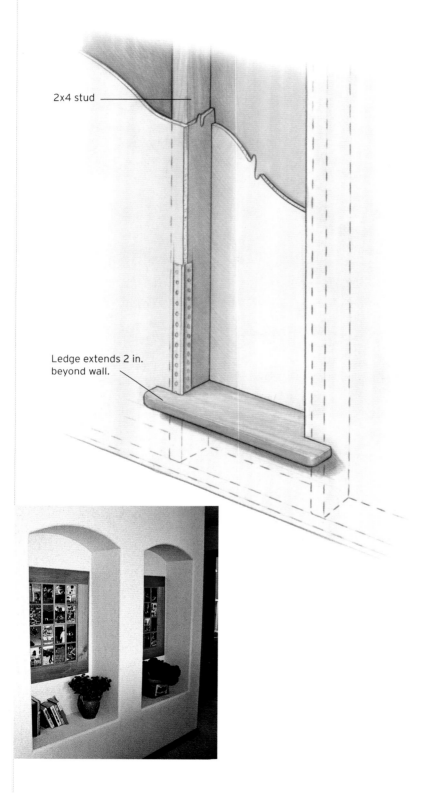

2x4 stud

Ledge extends 2 in. beyond wall.

the material of choice for ceiling and wall ornamentation. Drywall is plaster's modern-day descendent. It won't warp, dry out, crack, or pull loose. And unlike plaster, it's easy to work, requiring only a little practice rather than years of experience.

You can make trim boards of any width or shape just by slicing the desired dimension off a sheet of drywall. Build the trim up to the desired thickness by layering the sheets. To achieve an even edge, plane the sheet with a drywall rasp. Then use one of the hundreds of plastic trim profiles now available to craft a crisp border. The border can be finished to perfection with drywall compound and a little sanding.

Creating Nooks and Crannies

If you live in a wood-framed house, you have unexploited space right now between the studs of your interior walls. As you lay out a remodeling project, look for ways to build in art coves, recessed shelves, and storage spaces. Drywall simplifies the job: locate the studs, draw a nook between them, then use a drywall saw to remove the rectangle you've sketched. Inset wood blocks at the top and bottom of the opening. Wrap the sides of the nook with drywall. Finish by taping, sanding, and painting, and you're done. If the wall is only a standard 3½ in. thick, you might want to add a ledge that projects outward like a windowsill.

Frame a deeper nook by building a plywood box and inserting it between two studs. Anchor the box into the framing with screws. Use drywall corner bead to trim the joint between the wall and the box, finish the edges with drywall compound, and paint.

Easy Arches and Wraps

Creating an elegant archway once was a challenge, given the square edges of framing lumber and the rigidity of drywall. But with the flexible Archway Fast Cap™ (Trim-Tex® Drywall Products), you scribe the curve you want on the wall, cut the shape from both sides of the opening, and snap the Archway

Photo by: Larry Douglas

An inexpensive wood cap protects this stair railing from daily wear and tear.

cap into place. It's attached by stapling the cap's flange to the wall and then easily finish with drywall tape.

Resilient vinyl wall caps make short work of finishing off the top of stair rakes and drywall-wrapped openings. Without them, drywall tends to stain easily, and the traditional metal beads used for edging are susceptible to dents. Another option is to use a 1x4 jamb protector of wood or MDF, caulked into place.

BASEBOARDS AND CHAIR RAILS

Although drywall trim tends not to hold up well over time, you can combine it with solid trim for durability at a reasonable cost. Say you want 8-in.-high baseboards. Score and break off a strip of drywall that size, attach it to the wall, and cap it with rounded J-bead or cove molding. Next, layer a 4-in. stock baseboard over the drywall, as shown on p. 150.

Fast Cap Installation

There is no need for backing with drywall at the curves. Just cut the arch and install. Attach the Fast Cap, then finish with drywall compound around the edges.

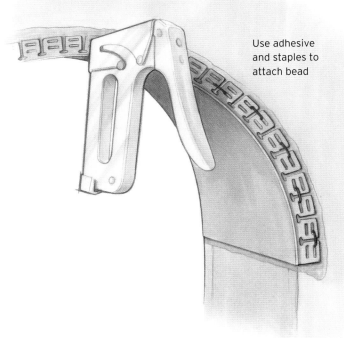

Use adhesive and staples to attach bead

Low-Cost Baseboard with High Impact

By layering strips of drywall and stock drywall moldings, you can have a tall, impressive baseboard without the cost of large wood moldings and a carpenter. The MDF bottom piece resists vacuum-cleaner bumps and shoe scuffs.

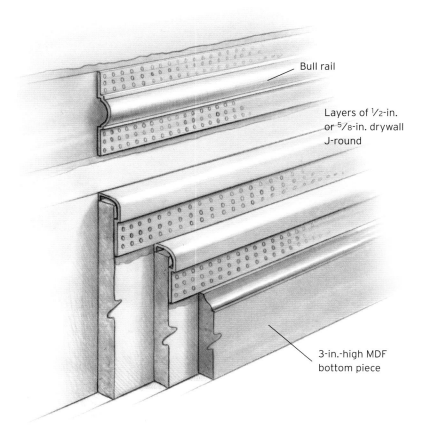

Bull rail

Layers of 1/2-in. or 5/8-in. drywall J-round

3-in.-high MDF bottom piece

Caulk along the joint between the drywall and the base, and finish with semigloss paint to create what will look like a tall, solid-wood baseboard, without the solid price.

You can quickly achieve the appearance of a chair rail with a technique commonly found in commercial construction. Use drywall channels to form an indent that creates a shadow line (or *reveal*) on the wall, rather than a protrusion. Begin by locating and drawing the shadow line at the desired height. With a drywall knife, score two parallel lines 3/8 in. apart and chisel out the loose material between. Next, set the bead into the kerf, and attach its flange to the wall with staples. Finish the edges with drywall compound, taking care not to fill in the notch.

Wainscoting

Wainscoting is a traditional wall treatment, typically consisting of three components: chair rail molding, base molding, and a series of panels in between. Today, plywood often is substituted for the panels, but even then wainscoting can be very expensive. Another way to go is to use paint-grade picture frame moldings to outline panel-size spaces and fill them in with wallpaper or paint.

If you prefer the classical look of wood paneling, buy inexpensive cabinet doors from a home center and set them within a frame of decorative molding that has a

If you anticipate that certain walls of the remodeled area of the house are apt to take a beating, you can protect their lower third with bead board wainscoting.

TRADE SECRET
WAINSCOTING 1-2-3

You can create the look of wainscoting simply by establishing rectangles with strips of molding. Begin by choosing a baseboard and chair rail to establish the top and bottom of the wainscoting. Then decide on a size for the wainscot panels. Cut a pattern for this rectangle out of cardboard or paper and trace its outline around the room. Make sure that the layout is visually pleasing. Then use stock door casing on four sides to create rectangles, similar to picture frames. Paint all the trim with enamel to highlight the effect.

grooved (or *rabbeted*) edge to fit over the door edges. Either use matching woods or pick up the least expensive materials you can find and paint the assembly.

For a less formal wainscoting, use bead board— traditionally, strips of narrow boards with beaded edges. However, you'll get the same look using plywood panels that have been cut with a beaded effect. To install the wainscoting, begin by carefully removing the baseboard. Cut the bead board to the desired height and attach it to the wall with finish nails and panel adhesive. Run panel molding along the top edge and reinstall the existing baseboard over the bead board.

The least expensive wainscot of all can be accomplished with a chair rail atop a deep, contrasting shade of paint or wallpaper.

Slightly more elaborate is using painter's tape to mask panel-like rectangles, then painting those areas with a rich, complementary color.

Unpredictable Partitions

You may find that remodeling brings out a quirky side in you that has gone unexpressed. Here is your chance to explore such modern techno-textures as corrugated tin roofing, metal laminates, plastics, and aluminum panels. Used confidently, these low-cost materials can create extraordinary effects. I once saw a designer install sheets of remnant plastic laminate on an accent wall, wrong side facing out. The surface suggested palm wood or walnut, for about 1 percent the price of the real thing.

Corrugated metal sheets lend industrial chic to a room. Instead of drywall, which covers walls throughout the house, or expensive stone facing, the corrugated metal adds contrast and visual interest.

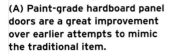
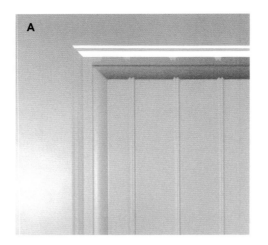

(A) Paint-grade hardboard panel doors are a great improvement over earlier attempts to mimic the traditional item.

(B) Imitation wood doors can be had in a variety of species, from oak to alder, and they look surprisingly authentic. Most visitors to your home will never know the difference.

Generous Molding

To inexpensively create the look of a wide, traditional-looking molding, case drywall-wrapped windows or doors with standard 2-in. paint-grade trim that's set back from the drywall edge. Paint the drywall jamb and casing to match other trim in the room.

INTERIOR DOORS AND TRIM

Because first impressions are so important in architecture, I recommend selecting the millwork you *really* want for the entry and walkways leading from it. In my house, I bought 7-ft. solid maple doors for the coat closet, basement, and powder room—the 3 doors visitors are most likely to see. The other 27 doors are two-panel embossed hardboard units that cost less than $50 each.

If you want wood doors throughout, an affordable solution is to buy prefinished veneered doors that have the traditional frame-and-panel appearance. The manufacturer may offer a line of matching casing and baseboard to complement the doors. Or, go with paint-grade doors that have a realistic imitation of wood grain. These are used even in high-end homes, and the styles include strikingly modern variations. Add warmth by trimming them with natural wood casing.

Disappearing Doors

If you don't have room for a regular door, such as for a small bathroom, consider a pocket door. They slide back into the wall and take up no extra room because they don't require the arc of a conventional hinged door.

Pocket doors were used in Victorian houses to close off rooms in a way that reconfigured

Pocket-Door Layouts

You can use a single pocket door as a doorway or two pocket doors as a retractable wall. In old houses, a single large room was often subdivided into two using a pair of pocket doors.

Single pocket door

Double pocket doors

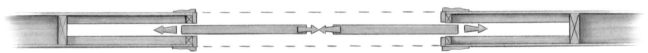

In a small house, pocket doors can mean the difference between doors and no doors. In some locations, there's simply not enough room to pare 9 sq. ft. for the door swing. The double pocket door shown here can also be the key to a flexible floor plan. When open, the room behind the doors becomes part of the adjacent area; when closed, the space becomes private.

Pocket doors come as a kit that includes a frame. After covering the frame with drywall, hang the door on the track and then attach the jamb stops to hold the door in place.

WHEN CHOOSING BASEBOARD, HEIGHT MAKES A GREATER IMPRESSION than thickness. If you are on a tight budget, select tall profiles on the thin side.

Compensate for the ordinariness of inexpensive paint-grade baseboards by choosing a profile that's a bit taller than standard trim.

Photo by: Jim Zack

the floor plan. You might install them so that a den doubles as a guest room, or so a portion of the family room can be set off as a formal dining area. In our home, we used three pocket doors to allow changing a hangout room for our teenagers into an occasional guest room for Grandma. This flexibility may make it unnecessary for you to build an addition to accommodate an infrequently used guest room.

Top-Flight Stairways

Stairways do more than go up and down. They represent the transition between public and private spheres: from the entry, living, and dining areas to bedrooms above. To dress up a staircase with inexpensive accents, try placing decorative ceramic tiles on the risers. Or use laminate plank flooring on

each riser and install fitted carpet on the treads to create the appearance of a solid wood stairway under a plush carpet runner.

You can give a stair wall an elegant look by using paint-grade casing to frame parallelograms as a sort of wainscoting. Simpler still, create these shapes with a contrasting color of satin or semigloss paint, guiding your work with a straightedge and masking tape.

FLOORING FUNDAMENTALS

Wood or stone flooring wears better and provides a more hygienic surface than carpeting. But wall-to-wall carpeting is the least expensive flooring for large areas and is comfortable underfoot. Before choosing, consider the options. If you decide on carpet, consider a low, tight nap for high-

Ready-made hardwood tread caps can be scribed to fit over the open end of treads or against the skirting. They give the impression of a solid wood stair with a carpet runner.

We coat plain $3/8$-in. parallel bars and commercial tubing with bronze metallic paint in constructing a strikingly modern staircase for a very affordable price.

SPLURGE A BIT WITH RELATIVELY EXPENSIVE MILLWORK IN THE ENTRYWAY, corridor, and living room, then switch to narrower moldings with the same profile in adjacent rooms and upstairs. To save even more, skip moldings altogether in closets, the laundry room, and utility areas.

PRO TIP

This stairway features painted poplar skirting with a corner molding. Note how the appearance of a carpet runner was created by installing a border of carpet with a contrasting texture.

By painting ordinary balusters with faux metallic paints, Heather Callam enlivened an otherwise plain stairway.

Combine plain balusters with a few fancy ones, and upgrade the look of a banister for a small incremental cost.

CARPETS THAT LAST

When choosing carpets, the bulkiest may not be the best. The least expensive varieties have stapled fibers and tend to fray more quickly, releasing fuzz when vacuumed. For more durability, look for the least expensive line of *continuous filament* nylon, even if it does not appear to be as full as some carpets with stapled fibers. Fiber can be deceiving. Longevity depends more on the fibers' length and twist than the total weight, or *plush*, of the carpet.

traffic areas, reserving plush carpeting for bedrooms and dens. Tightly bound carpets like wool berbers wear especially well and can be cleaned more thoroughly. Deeper piles tend to fray and work best in places where you might want to stretch out on the floor, such as in front of the TV. Although a thick, cushiony pad may make carpeting feel luxurious, you'll get more wear from the carpet if you use a dense padding.

Because carpeting in stairways and hallways tends to wear faster than in bedrooms and dens, I like to use a higher grade on these surfaces and shift to a less expensive choice in adjacent areas. If you use a similar color, the transition can be almost imperceptible.

Carpet tiles are increasingly popular. While they tend to be pricey compared to wall-to-wall carpet, you can easily install them. And there is little waste, because you buy just what you need rather than discarding big pieces from a roll of carpet. You might want to use them creatively, selecting two or more colors or styles to mix into a pattern.

Wood Floors

When remodeling, it may be difficult to install a new floor of ¾-in. hardwood if door thresholds, appliances, built-in cabinets, and other fixtures get in the way. Thinner options exist. The least expensive is plastic laminate flooring, available with excellent imitations of wood in a variety of species and tones. The material is tough, resists scratching, and never dulls or needs waxing. Generally, laminates cost about as much as medium-grade carpet. They are available in several quality levels, as reflected by guarantees as short as 5 years and as long as 20 years. Unless you install laminate in a low-traffic area, get a kind with at least an 8-year to 10-year warranty.

For somewhat more per square foot, you can have an engineered wood floor. These feature real wood laminated onto a wood or fiberboard core. They're sold in styles ranging from classic strip to distressed farmhouse plank, and in species from bamboo

A high-quality floor paint will serve well over old plank flooring, as shown, or over plywood sheathing for the most affordable type of flooring.

With flooring of solid wood, you can use contrasting species to create borders and patterns, as done here with white oak and mahogany inlay.

If you plan on using an attractive carpet in a room, consider installing hardwood flooring only around the perimeter.

YOU CAN INSTALL PLASTIC LAMINATE FLOORING ON A DRY SLAB, but any moisture wicking through concrete will damage the substrate. You are better off choosing a floor of engineered wood.

PRO TIP

This extraordinary surface is ordinary concrete, stained with an acid-reactive product and acrylic sealer. Polishing the surface with paste wax will add a burnished luster.

You may not have noticed, but vinyl flooring has been evolving. New products are hard wearing, easy to clean, warm underfoot, and eye catching in appearance.

You can now buy large squares of composition tile that contain a high percentage of limestone and are ready for installation over the existing underlayment. They look very much like the ceramic tile now in vogue.

to walnut. These floors typically are glued to the subfloor or sheathing. Expect to pay about as much as you would for a solid wood floor. Although the finish on an engineered floor is durable, the top wood layer may not be thick enough to allow refinishing. I recommend an engineered wood floor only if you cannot install ¾-in. boards, if the flooring is going over concrete, or if you want an exotic variety of wood unavailable in solid planks.

To save money on installing a hardwood floor, shop around for a lower grade of material. Buy 10 percent more than you need so that you can cull unusable planks; any boards that don't make the cut can be used in closets.

Other Hard Surfaces

Stone and tile can make hard-wearing, low-maintenance floors. But if they go over a wood-framed subfloor, be sure the underlying surface is stiff enough to prevent the floor from cracking. Masons once floated a concrete mortar bed as the tile base. The modern equivalent is concrete backer board. These boards are heavy and somewhat difficult to cut, but when used in combination with flexible acrylic mastics and epoxy grouts, they are rigid enough for most masonry products.

Stone and ceramic tile may be the floors of choice for the kitchen, bath, and entry. But for less than half the price of ordinary tile, you can have your choice of high-end vinyl flooring. If you've been unimpressed with vinyl in the past, check out the latest offerings. Manufacturers are developing new flooring palettes and patterns, just as they have for countertops. Your vinyl floor no longer has to look like you cut corners and remodeled on the cheap.

Linoleum is an old-time material that's back in vogue. The colors are rich, and they run through the sheets rather than being printed on them. Because it is largely made from linseed oil and cork, linoleum is thought of as "green" flooring. So are cork floors, which are available as tiles or in rolls. If you buy cork that's not prefinished, protect it with three or four coats of polyurethane. You can stain cork like wood (it *is* a form of wood, after all) or simply seal it.

A concrete floor calls to mind dank basements and oily garages. But concrete recently has been dressed up to become a popular flooring material for living areas as well. When polished with diamond grinders, stained with reactive chemicals, and sealed with acrylic, it can look much like glossy marble.

Design Plan in a Can

Those of us who struggle to color coordinate our wardrobes may be daunted by the options available in paint, flooring, cabinets, and countertops. And not everyone can afford the services of a professional interior designer.

Enter Edith Snell, a designer who has made decorating less precarious with her series of expertly coordinated samples of colors and materials, tidily tucked into a paint can. She also includes the "Color Placement Recommendation Guide" which gives detailed instructions for every room in the house, from floor to ceiling. The can is an alternative to the traditional designer board, a bulky display panel onto which color chips and product samples are glued. And instead of relying on exclusive, pricey designer lines, Snell selected her swatches from national brands available almost anywhere.

Her Design Plan in a Can™ series now includes more than 80 color palettes in eight collections that range from trendy island tones to classic neutrals and the timeless aesthetic of the Arts and Crafts movement. "I have worked at least 15 hours on choosing the elements in each can," says Snell, which translates into about $1,000 worth of design fees—for around one-tenth of the price.

Photo by: Edith Snell

If your decorating sense is less than infallible, these samples and swatches can save you from agonizing over picking tasteful combinations of color and texture when remodeling.

7

Affordable Kitchens and Baths

THE BEST REASON TO REMODEL A KITCHEN OR BATH-ROOM is because you want to, plain and simple. If you need to justify the expense, feel free to invoke "resale value," because you won't have trouble finding a remodeling contractor who will assure you that upgrading a kitchen will pay for itself several times over. But unless you got a bargain on a fantastic house in a wonderful neighborhood, and the kitchen is its only failing, you'll be lucky to break even. And the average return on a bathroom remodel is only marginally better.

It's particularly easy to overspend on kitchens because they contain all the most expensive elements in the house: plumbing, appliances, cabinets, countertops, lighting, and flooring. Every item presents myriad choices and oodles of upgrades. Remodeling this room on a budget is like dieting at an all-you-can-eat buffet.

Ritch Paprocki kept to a tight remodeling budget by installing ceramic tile countertops and refinishing hardwood floors himself. The drop ceiling was framed to define the adjacent dining room and conceal new ductwork.

PROFIT OR LOSS

According to *REALTOR® Magazine*, the average return on investment for a kitchen remodel ranges from 84 percent to 98 percent. If you think of your house as an investment, would you buy a stock that boasted a loss of 2 percent to 16 percent? In kitchen investments, the good news is that the less you spend, the higher the return. But unless you're in the kitchen-remodeling business, you shouldn't expect to make money. Expect instead to reap the enjoyment of a remodeled room.

PROJECT	JOB COST	RESALE VALUE	PERCENT OF COST RECOUPED AT SALE (NATIONAL AVERAGE)
Major kitchen remodel, upscale	$47,888	$69,194	84.8%
Major kitchen remodel, midrange	$43,862	$39,920	91%
Minor kitchen remodel	$14,913	$14,691	98.5%

Source: *REALTOR® Magazine.*

This beautiful kitchen would cost you a pretty penny with its European-style doors of glazed maple, dovetail-jointed drawer boxes, granite counters, an under-mount stainless steel sink, and hinged spiral knobs of real pewter. Yet you can have much the same look and feel with relatively inexpensive alternatives.

Stock builder-quality hardware has a pewterlike finish for about one-fifth the cost of the true pewter knobs.

Laminate counters have the look of granite but cost only about one-tenth as much as stone.

Look for bargains in the scratch and dent section of your appliance store. Because of a dent in a side panel (now hidden by the cabinet) this new stove from Sears® sold for one-third its original price at a Sears Appliance Outlet.

KITCHENS A CUT ABOVE

Now for the good news. Although the average kitchen remodel currently costs something over $45,000, you can do a lot more for a lot less, as this chapter will demonstrate. Kitchens don't need to be expensive to be beautiful and impressive.

Thumb through home magazines for inspiration, and you're likely to find glossy photos of a kitchen full of good-looking people wearing haute couture, sipping red wine, and leaning on granite countertops. Your own kitchen may seem humble and hopeless in comparison. Instead of tearing out your cabinets (or your hair), take stock. Consider subtle upgrades that might make a radical kitchenectomy unnecessary. Begin by reviewing how you might transform this room by accessorizing and adding just a few new pieces.

A good strategy for remodeling a kitchen affordably is to focus on function and use. Think of your kitchen as a workplace and get appliances that are priced according to how you use them and how often you use them. That may mean buying from the low end of what's on the market. Or if you enjoy cooking and entertaining on a big scale, you might consider commercial-grade equipment. I jokingly refer to my wife's high-end eight-burner gas stove as her table-saw because it is made for serious kitchen duty. But this appliance isn't an idle luxury because she cooks three meals daily and restaurant-style dinners at least once a week. The stove corresponds with her cooking needs, not her vanity. On the other hand, while we might have chosen an exotic stone

Redirecting Traffic

Sometimes all it takes to improve a kitchen is redirecting traffic around the cook. By adding an island as a traffic median, the person with the sharp knives and hot pans can work uninterrupted.

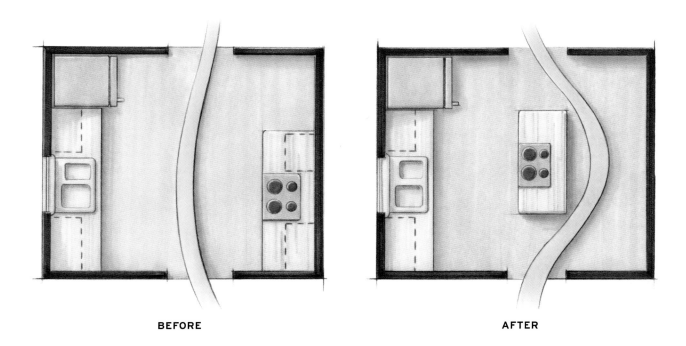

BEFORE   **AFTER**

for our ample countertops, we saved by going with Formica®, and the cabinets are stock items.

Redirecting Traffic

Start by drawing a plan of your existing kitchen, highlighting work areas and traffic patterns. Do people pass through the room in a way that interrupts the activity? If so, see if you can rearrange the kitchen—and don't feel obliged to think in terms of the familiar "work triangle" between the stove and refrigerator and sink. This is an old formula that may make sense if you live alone, but it's too simplistic a model for a busy household.

You may want to place the refrigerator outside of the work triangle so that others can rummage around in it without bother-

ing the cook. Nor does the sink have to be in the thick of things if an automatic dishwasher spares you from spending a lot of time in the suds. Map out a new layout in terms of *zones*—an area for cleaning, another for chopping, and a captain's bridge at the stove. For most households, the stove should be at the center, with easy access to the sink and a countertop for chopping and piling ingredients.

Next, think about storage. Specifically, look for ways to stash things somewhere other than the kitchen. If you have a nearby laundry, back porch, or garage, give some thought to remodeling a section of this space into a pantry. By adding a generous pantry lined with simple shelving, you'll be able to rip out cabinets that now make the kitchen feel cramped. In their place,

1. Determine the cook's busiest hub and deflect traffic away from it.

2. Place the refrigerator where others can use it without colliding with the cook.

3. Design separate satellite stations for food preparation, stovetop cooking, cleaning, and hanging out.

4. Install two kinds of lighting: task and ambient.

5. Plan for more counter space than you think you'll need.

6. Provide ventilation, including both operable windows and an exhaust fan.

7. Build in more than one roll-out waste container to encourage your kitchen assistants to clean up after themselves.

An out-of-the-way storage area for appliances, holiday tableware, or dry goods can free up cabinet space in the kitchen. Open shelves were used here instead of upper cabinets, for a bistro look on a budget.

Think Outside the Triangle

The traditional efficiency triangle had space for only one cook and didn't include any helpers or observers. Depending on how your household operates, it may be more realistic to arrange the kitchen with a spouse, kids, and visitors in mind.

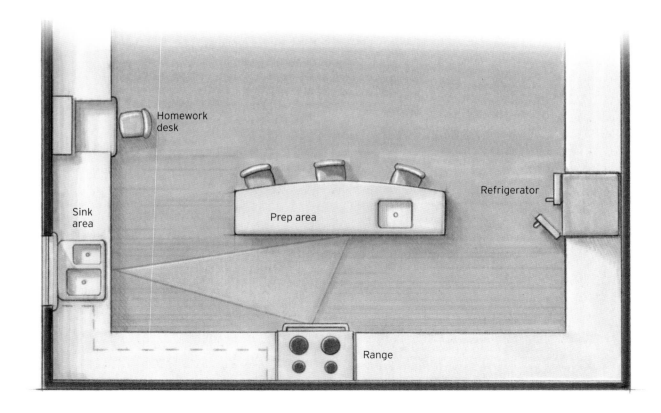

Homework desk

Sink area

Prep area

Refrigerator

Range

NEED SOME ADVICE ON HOW TO BRING ALL THE PIECES INTO A HARMONIOUS WHOLE? Some cabinet stores have designers on staff who can help you lay out your kitchen free of charge.

add a window, open shelves, a wine rack, or artwork. The result will be that your kitchen looks bigger and brighter, possibly sparing you the expense of building a new one.

Nowadays the cook is often the life of the party, which means you may want room for guests to congregate in the kitchen (without getting in the way). Islands and peninsulas work wonderfully for these informal groupings, but if you don't have room for either, consider a narrow wall-mounted bar.

CABINET CONSERVATION

New cabinets can make up a third of the cost of a typical kitchen remodeling, so it pays to explore alternatives to replacing them. The options include refacing, painting, and accessorizing. Even if you know you need new cabinets, consider just replacing door and drawer fronts. The "wow factor" with new cabinets involves new finishes, trim details, and storage features, and these can be added to existing cabinets.

If you have a vintage home, you may want to preserve a part of its architectural history by keeping at least a few of the original cabinets—fronts and all—and using them to set a remodeling theme. Keep in mind that period architecture remains timeless, while a trendy remodel is apt to date your house quickly. Today's fashion has a way of becoming tomorrow's avocado nightmare.

New door and drawer fronts and a relaminated countertop can transform an old, musty kitchen into a showpiece.

AFTER

BEFORE

If time and money are tight, I recommend postponing work on the cabinet exteriors, along with adding new countertops and a backsplash. Instead, concentrate for now on improving the function of these storage areas. The details can come later.

It's What's Inside That Counts

You now can buy an impressive array of handy spice racks, pull-out cutting boards, tray racks, sponge trays, appliance garages, and even a recycling center with separator bins. Most of this hardware can be mounted on exiting cabinets.

■ **Shelf drawers** are perhaps the most useful storage feature you can add, making good use of the space deep within the cabinet.

■ **Drawer organizers** include multilevel versions that take advantage of deep old-style drawers, which otherwise collect a jumble of odds and ends.

■ **Roll-out trash trolleys** can be installed in base cabinets where the shelving isn't being fully used.

■ **Tilt-out sink trays** make use of the shallow space behind the decorative panels in

Mixing, not matching, is the key to adding new cabinets. In this kitchen, painted wood cabinets work to complement. A vintage stove manages to look appropriate next to the stainless steel refrigerator. Note that, in a break with standard practice, there are no upper cabinets, just an open shelf.

If your kitchen is chronically short on storage space, look into the remarkable array of options for making better use of every square inch.

A professional stainless steel pot rack suspends a couple of cupboards worth of cookware. It also drops the hint that a serious gourmet cook is in the house.

front of the kitchen sink. The trays are the perfect place to tuck sponges, sink stoppers, and scouring brushes.

■ **Appliance lifts** save counter space by allowing you to mount a food processor or other appliance on a platform that mounts on the back of a cabinet door. The lift raises the appliance to counter height and locks in the open position.

■ **Appliance garages** can be used to hide countertop clutter behind a roll-up door. They are installed between the countertop and the wall cabinet above and may have a handy electrical outlet inside so that appliances can be kept plugged in.

■ **Rails and pot racks** are installed against a wall or hang from the ceiling to store all

manner of things that otherwise would take up counter and cabinet space. Commercial-duty racks suggest you have a professional expertise in the kitchen, whether or not that is the case.

These storage devices are widely available at home centers, at cabinet shops, and through the Internet. The necessary hardware will be included, and most can be installed with just a drill and screwdriver.

Replace the Moving Parts

Hinges and drawer slides are the first parts to wear out on kitchen cabinets. You can easily replace them with hardware every bit as good as that in new cabinetry.

You may find that the screw holes for

INSTALLING CABINET DOORS MAY TAKE A FEW TRIES.
To make the process of fitting hinges and aligning doors less frustrating, install only one screw in each hinge until everything lines up perfectly, then drive in the rest of the screws.

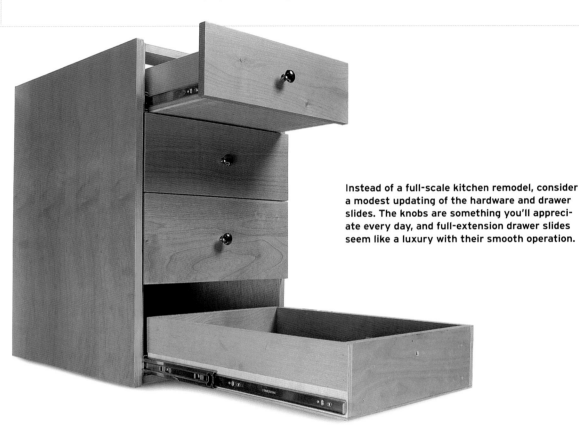

Instead of a full-scale kitchen remodel, consider a modest updating of the hardware and drawer slides. The knobs are something you'll appreciate every day, and full-extension drawer slides seem like a luxury with their smooth operation.

hinges have become too large over time. If so, you should be able to firmly anchor replacement hinges by moving them up or down ¼ in. or so. Just make sure that you don't install a pair of new hinges that are obviously out of alignment with the rest. Another option is to fill in the old screw holes. Put dabs of carpenter's glue on the ends of wooden toothpicks or matchsticks, insert them in the holes, let dry, break off the tips and drive home the screws. If the door sits flush with the cabinet frame rather than overlapping it, you have the option of using a face-mounted hinge instead of the conventional sort.

New drawer glides are a revelation if you've been living with stubborn drawers.

You will find a range of products from plastic friction tracks to ball-bearing hardware. I prefer ball-bearing face-frame brackets that mount on either side of the drawer, like those used for file cabinets. They provide good support when fully extended and won't bind. Although they can be relatively expensive, you'll spend less for them than you would for new cabinets. Or you can buy a good-quality single slide for about half as much as a side-mounted pair.

PAINT, REFACE, OR REPLACE

One nice thing about painted cabinetry is that you can keep up with changing trends in home decor simply by repainting. But

A row of tomato-red cabinets highlights a small but adventuresome remodel. In terms of appeal, style can usually trump size and cost.

A quick and easy way to give cabinets an antique glazed look is to darken the kerf along crown molding or door panels with a black indelible marker.

You can revive your tired kitchen cabinets by refinishing them for a contemporary look. Glazed cream tones with an antiqued patina have become very popular.

rather than just making the cabinets look freshly painted, antique the surface by sanding away the finish along edges that would be expected to receive wear.

If You Prefer Wood

If you have stained-wood cabinets that look a little scruffy, they may just need cleaning with a good furniture cleaner. After removing two or three decades of grease, grime, and dulled varnish, you might discover the cabinets don't need anything but a fresh coat of polyurethane. But if the cabinets have been finished with either shellac or lacquer, you should stay with that product when refinishing. To test the compatibility of a finish, try applying it to a small and inconspicuous area. If you want to be less involved, you can

remove the cabinet doors and drawer faces for professional refinishing, then concentrate on doing just the face frames.

Whether you stain or paint your old cabinets, you can take advantage of the opportunity to dress up the doors and boxes with molding. This can do a lot to improve the appearance of the plain plywood doors that first made their appearance in the 1940s. For example, you might use casing or bead molding around the perimeter of the doors to suggest traditional frame-and-panel construction.

Putting on a New Face

The equivalent to cosmetic surgery in kitchen remodeling is cabinet refacing. The procedure typically involves replacing the kitchen

Dress Up a Door

Birch plywood cabinet doors have been a standard in countless kitchens, and if they still remain serviceable, you can update their flat panel doors by routing out the middle of each and inserting a thin beadboard panel.

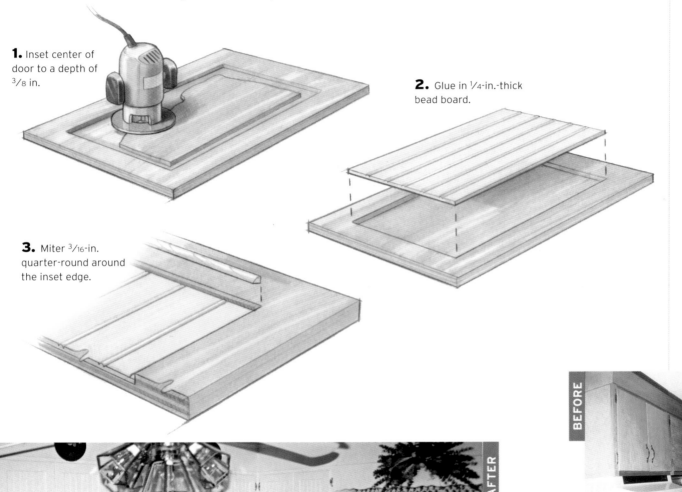

1. Inset center of door to a depth of ³/₈ in.

2. Glue in ¹/₄-in.-thick bead board.

3. Miter ³/₁₆-in. quarter-round around the inset edge.

BEFORE

AFTER

Homeowner Tom Reeves used a router with a straight bit to make a recess in these old cabinet doors, then inserted bead board framed by ³/₁₆-in. quarter-round molding. Paint, new hardware, and plastic-laminate countertops completed the update.

AFTER

If you're happy with your kitchen layout, refacing might be all you need. Here's an example of how old cabinets can be brought back to life with new doors, drawer fronts, veneered face frames and sides, and hardware, as well as a valance over the window and crown molding used to scribe the soffit.

BEFORE

Cabinet Refacing

If your cabinets still function well but look tired, consider replacing just the doors and drawer fronts. Paint or veneer the face frame and end panels, either trying for a close match, or coming up with a complementary finish.

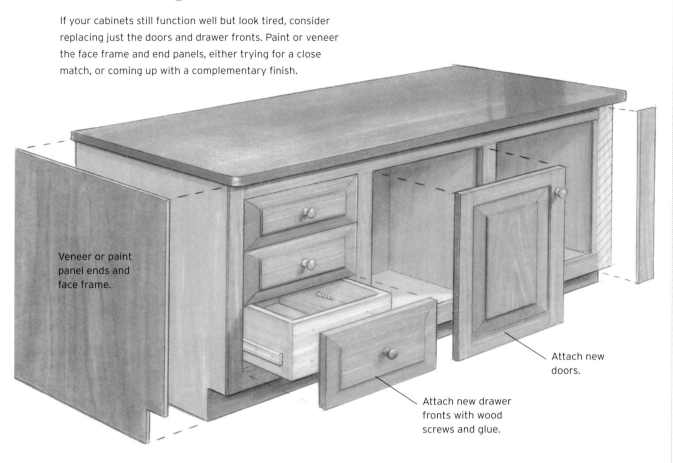

Veneer or paint panel ends and face frame.

Attach new doors.

Attach new drawer fronts with wood screws and glue.

doors and drawer fronts and veneering the exposed cabinet face frames and ends. You can find specialty contractors who will do the job for 30 percent to 60 percent less than the cost of replacing the cabinets. Save still more by doing the job yourself. Most kitchen show-rooms and large home improvement chains will sell you the doors, drawer fronts, and materials you'll need. The work will go more easily if you merely paint the boxes before replacing doors and drawers, rather than veneering or refinishing them.

Whatever the cabinet style, the right knobs, pulls, and handles can elevate them above the ordinary. There are new styles as well as reproductions, but also consider visiting an antiques store or architectural salvage yard to look through their odds and ends.

Accessorize

Whatever the era or style and whether painted, refaced or new, your cabinets gain a jewelry-like sparkle and custom appeal by their knobs, pulls, and handles. Accessories can also make an ordinary finish look extraordinary. Choose from among wood, metal, porcelain, rubber, resins, stone, and even glass. Combine multiple materials to create a modulated, furniture-like appearance.

Although cheap by kitchen remodeling standards, knobs can cost more than you might expect. The $1,600 price tag for the knobs (not counting installation) in our kitchen made me postpone the purchase for several months. But sometimes the secret to less-expensive accessorizing lies in looking

Use a homemade template for fast, accurate knob placement.

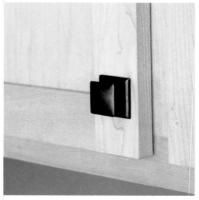

Knobs, pulls, and handles can have a surprisingly significant impact on your kitchen remodeling budget, but they are one of the easiest add-ons to save for later.

at things differently. You might find a set of pull handles that look almost exactly like the expensive ones you want, but in a package labeled "towel bars" and costing under $100. As mentioned earlier, search antiques stores and architectural salvage yards, where you can often find period cabinet pulls.

And consider trim, such as crown molding applied to the top and bottom of cabinets, as another accessory. For less than $3 per door, you can buy precut French provincial molding to dress up plain cabinet doors. For less than $50 a length, you can buy country valances to sandwich between cabinets or to set off a bank of open shelves, achieving a more traditional finish. A few lengths of gallery molding could dress up the top of your cabinets for under $100.

The gallery molding does not cost less than crown molding, but it's a lot easier to install. Split rope, dentil, fluted moldings, and split dowels—available from any lumberyard—can dress up an old kitchen as well as a new one built from inexpensive, stock cabinets. Accessories add high-end detailing at low cost, especially when you consider installing these several months or years after completing the original work. Planning this way allows you to opt for less costly material without feeling as if you were settling for less.

COMPLETE CABINET OVERHAUL

Replacing all your cabinets and countertops is the most expensive approach to a kitchen remodel, but even then you can save money and enjoy a kitchen that delivers more form and function than you paid for. When designing a replacement, don't overlook the obvious fact that the more individual cabinets you want, the more you'll spend. So try to reduce the number of cabinets it takes to complete one run. In other words, a single 48-in. cabinet will cost less than two 24-in. units.

Also expect solid-wood doors to cost more than veneered. Certain popular wood species, such as hickory and cherry, come at a premium.

ONCE YOU HAVE SETTLED ON A KITCHEN LAYOUT, PRICE THE CABINETS with several suppliers. Nearly identical lines of cabinets can have strikingly dissimilar price tags.

Jean and Paul Essman had their hearts set on granite countertops, but they weren't willing to sacrifice upgraded appliances and a butler's pantry to get them. Contractor Roger Reynolds suggested the Wilsonart® Deep Star Fossil pattern laminate shown here. With its beveled edge and textured surface, this surface comes close enough to satisfy the couple's craving for stone.

It takes a bit of nerve to combine disparate styles, but the effect can be energizing. Here, Arts and Crafts cabinets stand above a starkly Modern sink.

Photo by: Larry Douglas

Adding just a single custom cabinet can lift a remodeling out of the ordinary, as was done with this kitchen.

A professional kitchen remodeler makes the job look easy, thanks in part to thousands of dollars worth of tools. You may save money in the long run by forgoing the tool-buying spree and having cabinets installed for you, then taking over for the finishing touches.

But you can have relatively inexpensive birch and poplar in a variety of attractive finishes. Also have a look at less familiar woods, such as bamboo, wenge, Brazilian cherry (or jatoba), rubber tree hardwood, and Lyptus® (a eucalyptus hybrid grown in ecologically managed forests in Brazil.)

For the least-expensive option, turn to ready-to-assemble cabinets. They aren't difficult to put together with ordinary hand tools. Or pick up fully assembled stock cabinets in standard sizes from a home improvement center. And there's no need to use only one type of cabinet. Use stock factory-made products for most of the kitchen, then splurge on one or two custom-made pieces to take the room up a notch.

Skimp on Anything but Labor

Cabinet installation and related trim carpentry require specialized tools and years of practice. Hire the best installer you can find. The job is especially tricky in an older home, because the room's surfaces are apt to be out of level and may need work before installation.

If leveling the entire ceiling seems like too much of a project, consider installing recessed soffits over the upper cabinets. They are set in slightly from the front edge of the cabinets, unlike conventional soffits, which extend beyond the edge. Run crown molding along the top of the cabinets and between the soffit and ceiling. These recessed soffits will make the kitchen cabinets appear tall, slender, and more elegant. If you cut windowlike lighted nooks into the soffit as display areas, the effect can be striking.

Another way to make an uneven ceiling less conspicuous is to change the elevation of the wall cabinets. Raise one or two above the rest, and you'll also create a rhythmic break in a line of cabinets that might otherwise seem monotonous.

Floors and ceilings aren't likely to be the only challenges in an older house. Take into account that the corners of the kitchen may not be square and that factory cabinets and

Inset Soffit

Recessed soffits have a refined look when trimmed at the top and bottom with crown molding.

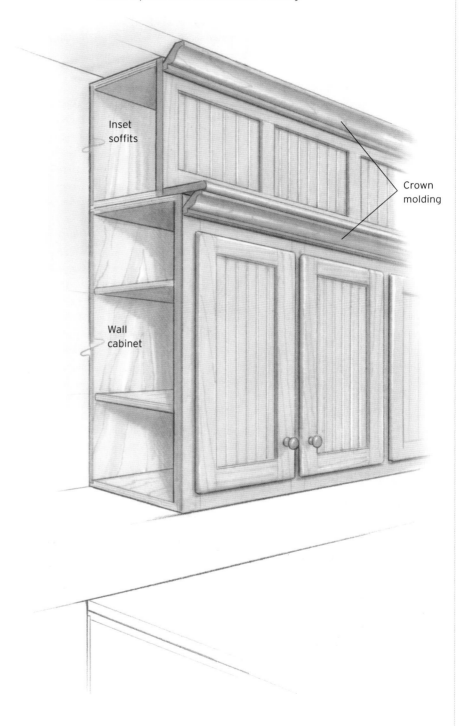

Inset soffits

Crown molding

Wall cabinet

For more counter space and to add an attractive variation, you can pull out a base cabinet 6 in. to 8 in. beyond the adjacent cabinets and cover the splice between the boxes with an angled piece of trim or a table leg.

By varying the horizontal and vertical alignment of cabinets, you add interest at virtually no extra cost.

This kitchen island was crafted in a straightforward way from four stock cabinets, a shelf, and two turned legs.

Big Island from Small Parts

By assembling a quartet of base cabinets, you can build a furniture-like island that provides the kitchen with cabinets, shelves, and a sitting area at one end. Table legs can be made with newel posts from the lumberyard.

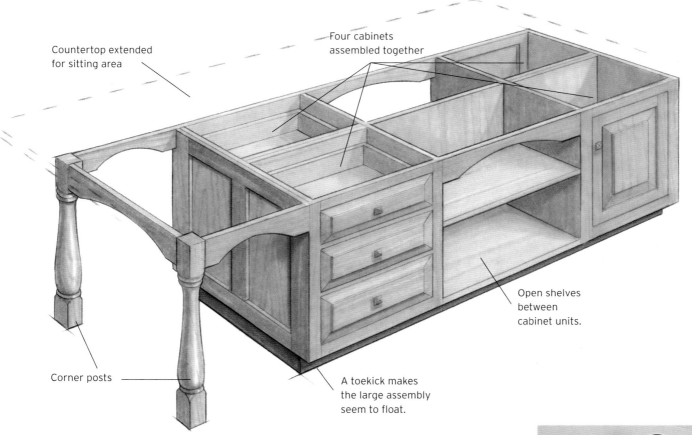

Countertop extended for sitting area

Four cabinets assembled together

Open shelves between cabinet units.

Corner posts

A toekick makes the large assembly seem to float.

countertops are unforgiving in that regard. You can compensate by pulling a cabinet away from the wall, putting an extra-wide panel on the end, and having a custom-fabricated countertop scribed to fit. But to avoid surprises, have a good installer review your kitchen plans and measure the existing space before placing an order.

Easy Extras

A few fancy tricks of the trade can add pizzazz at little or no cost. For a furniture-like finish, dress up the raw edge of a base cabinet with a pilaster that looks like a cabinet leg—newel posts work great—and then add an

arched toe kick, available at cabinet retailers.

For a good-size island at a reasonable cost, begin with one or two stock sink-base cabinets and back them up with 12-in.-deep wall cabinets for dish storage. You can raise the wall cabinets as needed on a toe kick, or buy 42-in.-tall wall cabinets to create a stool-height bar top.

Appliance garages are useful for concealing clutter, but they are expensive and may not have enough space for all your kitchen gadgets. Another way to create countertop storage is to mount standard 18-in.-high doors with the pivot slides used for entertainment center cabinets. This hardware allows doors to

To create a large storage area for countertop appliances, fit an entertainment center cabinet with pivot-slide doors.

OPEN SHELVES ARE A LOW-COST FORM OF STORAGE, providing easy access to dishes, glassware, cookbooks, and serving pieces. By not buying the doors of standard cabinets, you can cut the price by about a third.

Cabinets Put to Useful Ends

Try placing a wall cabinet at the end of an island or peninsula cabinet termination to add a little extra storage for cookbooks, wine bottles, or display items. Use door blanks to finish the exposed sides.

Wall cabinet added to end, with door blanks and side storage.

Photo courtesy of Miracle Method, Inc.

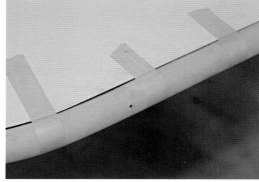

Refinishing companies can recoat an old countertop to look like seamless granite at less cost than recovering your counters with new laminate.

swing open 90 degrees, then slide back inside the cabinet and out of the way. To build an appliance garage, install two plywood cabinet sides, 24 in. apart, between the countertop and the upper cabinets. Cover the edges with a 2-in. face frame, and mount a pair of 12-in.-wide doors with these pivot slides.

A corner cabinet with a built-in lazy Susan is thought of as a space saver, but actually it wastes space on both sides of it. I suggest butting up the corners of the two perpendicu-lar cabinets and forget about the hollow space left in the blind corner. Add bracing along the wall to support the countertop in this area.

Wall cabinets, which are only 12 in. deep, can get you out of a tight spot. Use slender wall cabinets for your lower cabinets if you need a narrow storage bank where full depth cabinets would eliminate circulation area, such as in a galley kitchen or small laundry. Wall cabinets also provide design flexibility when planning and constructing islands and peninsulas. Consider using a wall cabinet at the end of a kitchen peninsula to extend the counter or to add a decorative end to a seating area. Wall cabinets are less expensive than lowers and, used creatively, can give a custom look to a kitchen built with stock cabinets. Use door fronts to trim the sides.

Cabinets traditionally sit up on a toekick, which provides room for your feet when you belly up to the counter. But this recess isn't necessary, and, in fact, cabinets built a 100 years ago didn't have one. If you're tight on drawer space, consider using full 36-in.-tall drawer banks that sit right on the floor instead of on a platform, giving you an extra ½ ft. of storage.

COUNTER INTELLIGENCE

If you think of countertops as simply work surfaces, you may save money by using plas-tic laminates. But most of us like to indulge in a little luxury. You might want to splurge on granite for an island or a small pastry station, while installing more strictly utilitar-ian surfaces elsewhere. There's no decorat-ing canon that says all the countertops in a kitchen have to be the same material.

Each material has its advantages and draw-backs. You might choose wood counters for around the stove, where you can set out hot pots and chop parsley. Metal, solid-surface, or plastic laminates serve well around the sink. Consider concrete, soapstone, marble, onyx, or tile on an island or bar or for an attractive backsplash.

By shopping through the Internet, you can find dramatic, no-nonsense com-mercial laminate counters as an alternative to the more common choices.

Baking Table

A baking table provides a good place to showcase a small but beautiful slab of granite or marble. Its lower height is ideal for kneading dough. At a home center, buy a stock desk-drawer unit and two newel posts (also called banister posts). Attach the drawer unit to the wall with screws, installing it between two base cabinets as shown.

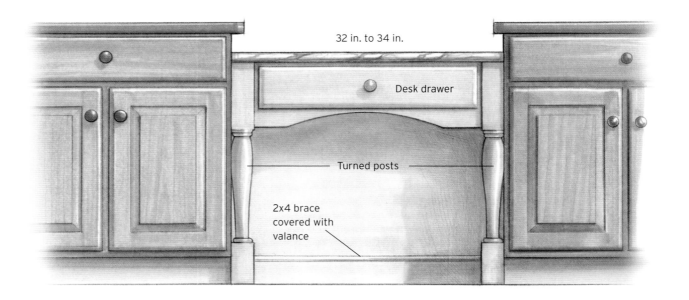

32 in. to 34 in.

Desk drawer

Turned posts

2x4 brace covered with valance

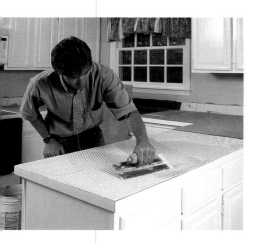

By using cement board, you can install ceramic tile without having to remove the countertop, saving a bit of money and a lot of time and bother.

■ **Wood** counters may be vulnerable to water, burns, and scratches, but as with wood floors, they can be kept looking new by refinishing. A high-quality wood counter will cost more than laminates or ceramic tile, but a lot less than granite.

■ **Tiles** come in a vast range of colors and materials, including cut stone, metal, glass, porcelain, and ceramic. Large pieces have become popular, and 24-in.-deep tiles allow you to do the entire length of a countertop one tile at a time. Tile is heatproof, scratch resistant, long lasting, and relatively inexpensive. Installing it is within the ability of the average handy homeowner. You can place tile over square-edged plastic laminate counters by first gluing and screwing ¼-in. cement tile backer board to the old surface. Above the counter, tile can be glued directly to the wall as a backsplash.

■ **Linoleum** on a countertop? It once was commonly used that way, taking advantage of the leftover scraps of flooring. These pieces just happen to correspond to the size of the counters for which the cuts were made.

■ **Plastic laminates** have been the best-selling countertop surface for more than 50 years. There's even nostalgia for the older styles, and you again can buy 1950s-patterned plastic with metal edging. If you want the laminate to look like something more expensive, consider a finish that mimics stone.

■ **Stainless steel** is nonporous, doesn't chip or scratch, and requires minimal maintenance. Its cost is between plastic laminates and granite. Along with heavy-duty pot racks and a massive stove, stainless-steel counters convey the impression that serious cooking

Varnished wood counters have long been a popular kitchen surface. Today, you can find them in species such as Honduran mahogany (shown here), environmentally benign Wood Welded® Lyptus, and traditional maple butcher block. An advantage of wood is that a scratched counter can be sanded and refinished to look as good as new.

New plastic laminates include beautiful, sophisticated surfaces such as this acid-etched metallic effect manufactured by Chemetal®.

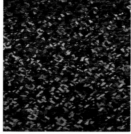

This festive pattern from Nevamar® recalls the glory days of plastic laminate, when people would tear out marble counters to replace them with an Art Deco surface.

goes on here. As an alternative, zinc and copper are softer than stainless steel and develop a patina of different tones as they age.

■ **Glass** is a nonporous surface that remains stainproof and hygienic. It can handle hot pots, and it's out of the ordinary. By placing ⅜-in.-thick plate glass over an attractive and unusual laminate, you will achieve an effect greater than the sum of the inexpensive materials. Consider using reeded, heat-deformed, etched, or glue-chip glass to refract light in dynamic ways.

■ **Solid synthetic surfaces,** such as Du-Pont® Corian®, don't have visible seams and can come close to the look of granite. They also come in highly inventive patterns that don't seek to reproduce anything under the sun. Because you can sand out scuffs and scrapes, the countertops are more durable

The backsplash on this countertop was made with Marmoleum® linoleum left over from the flooring installation.

TO BRING A LAMINATE COUNTERTOP OUT OF THE ORDINARY, add a 2-in. strip of hardwood edging.

Photo courtesy of Karran

You can mount a sink under a laminate counter for a look virtually indistinguishable from a solid-surface acrylic top. The sink has a special lip that glues directly to the laminate from below the counter surface. Installers trim the edge with a laminate router and polish it for a seamless fit.

TRADE SECRET
EASY COUNTERTOP MAKEOVER

For a truly inexpensive solution, consider having your laminate tops professionally refinished with a speckled paint that looks like granite or soapstone. The cost runs about half that of replacing the countertops altogether, and the finish can be expected to last roughly 10 years.

than laminates. You can save by using ¼-in.-thick material over a substrate, rather than buying standard ½-in. countertops.

■ **Alternative countertops.** Some of the newer surfaces offer an unusual look at prices below high-end products. Paper-based countertops by Richlite® provide a durable-as-stone, heat- and stain-resistant surface that has been used in commercial kitchens for years. Concrete is in vogue for countertops, and installers charge a lot for it. But you can make your own and stand a good chance of getting attractive results. It's best to experiment by creating a small surface, such as an outdoor counter or bar top, before tackling an entire kitchen. One method is to form and pour the concrete in place,

right on top of the base cabinets; the other is to pour the concrete into a mold and then install it over the cabinets, as you would granite or marble. Generally, pigmenting the concrete yields less reliable results than applying a stain to the surface.

Backsplashes

A backsplash serves the practical function of protecting the wall behind the counter, and it also gives you an opportunity to use a high-impact accent at a low cost. Because this surface doesn't get much wear, you can choose among materials that might be too delicate for a countertop, such as glass tile, holographic laminates, and metallic tile. We recently finished our kitchen backsplash

Photo by: Kevin Dwarka

Stainless steel, copper, and other nonrusting metals are serviceable and look good at a below-marble price.

A thick sheet of plate glass can enhance the look of any number of countertop materials while protecting the finish.

SIMPLE CONCRETE COUNTERTOP

If you want to try making a countertop of concrete, it's best to start with a modest-size project.

1. To make the bottom of the form, cut the shape for the countertop out of $3/4$-in.-thick melamine-coated particleboard. Build sides out of particleboard ripped to 2-in.-wide strips. Join the sides to the bottom and to each other at the corners with drywall screws. Fortify the slab with diamond mesh lath and sections of $1/8$-in. reinforcing set in 2 in. from the edges, corners, and sink cutout.

2. Prepare concrete to a stiff paste and trowel it into the mold, being careful to fill any voids. Tamp the concrete with a magnesium float, then work the surface with a wood float until smooth. Allow the counter to sit 1 hour, then finish with a steel trowel to seal the surface. Cover with damp burlap.

3. After five days to seven days, remove the concrete from the mold and place the slab on sawhorses. If the surface is too rough, burnish it with a diamond grinding wheel, then polish with it a random-orbit sander and 100-grit sandpaper. Wear a respirator to avoid inhaling the silica particles. You can also top the surface with a thin mix of compound or a mixture of mortar mix and latex additive mixed to the consistency of shaving cream. Skim the surface with a rubber trowel, working the mix into any voids or pockmarks. Screed off and then, after allowing the topping to dry a couple of days, sand again.

4. Clean the slab with a diluted solution of muriatic acid and rinse well. After the slab has air dried, color it with a reactive acid-etch concrete stain. Finish with water-based epoxy or, for the brightest results, solvent-based acrylic. Fasten the slab to the cabinet with adhesive caulk.

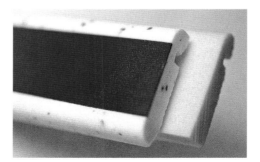

Kuehn™ Bevel manufactures an edging that you can apply to a standard laminate countertop to make it appear to be a solid material.

Frank Karreman, an architect on Bainbridge Island, Wash., stripped the plastic laminate from his counters, installed a layer of expanded wire lath, and created bullnose-edged forms with split PVC pipe. He then spread floor topping compound to build a thin concrete surface. The leather-like finish was created by staining the surface with several cups of black coffee, followed by a water-based floor sealer. The total cost was less than $100.

Honed stone counters come in 14-in. by 25-in. segments that glue onto a new or existing countertop in the manner of setting tile. A color-matching seam sealer finishes the installation. The cost is about that for ceramic tile.

Phenolic resin surfaces have a warm, natural appearance that comes from blending resin with paper, hemp, and other wood and plant products. The material is waterproof, sanitary, and strong. You can even sand the surface lightly and renew it with a coat of mineral oil, tung oil, or linseed oil.

Decorative tiles can add a custom look and a splash of color. On a backsplash, the job is limited enough in scale for a 17-year-old, like my son, to install.

These glass mosaic tiles come from Hakatai Enterprises, a company that encourages you to design your own patterns. You chose up to 10 colors, giving the percentage you need of each to make the design. An online preview screen lets you see the result before you order.

using delicate, iridescent mosaic glass tile from a company that lets you mix and match your own tapestry of mosaic for a personal look.

REDECORATE WITH THE FLICK OF A SWITCH

What's the easiest way to upgrade a kitchen? Improve the lighting. Because this is a work area, you need plenty of illumination in the form of both ambient and task lighting. Particularly helpful would be under-cabinet lights, which are easy to install. An electrician can take power from a nearby plug and surface-mount the wiring.

For overhead task and ambient lights, take advantage of an existing ceiling junction box to install track lighting, with pendants and spots that illuminate every corner. To add new ceiling lights, choose simple

chandeliers rather than recessed can lights. Can lights have a couple of strikes against them in a remodel. They are more difficult and expensive to retrofit, requiring you to cut holes in the drywall, and they cast only a small pool of light.

WATERWORKS

If you love to cook, it's important to have a sink that lets you submerge a big pot. Gourmet kitchen sinks hearken back to the old days, with bowls more generously sized than the commonplace 7½-in.-deep builder model. The least expensive gourmet sinks are dense acrylic composites with finishes from dull porcelain to granite. Slightly less expensive than a traditional cast-iron sink, they won't chip and are resilient enough to spare a dish that happens to slip from soapy hands.

A well-lighted kitchen plays up the best features of your remodel and also makes it easier and safer to work.

To maximize useful space, the bowls of this two-compartment model from Koehler have squared edges.

SINKAGE

Your best choice in an affordable kitchen sink is a good-quality stainless steel. Stay away from sinks with shallow bowls and thin-gauge walls. They aren't durable and will rattle annoyingly when you turn on the garbage disposer. Also, the shiny finish will come off if you attempt to clean the metal with steel wool—and then they'll rust. If you're going to buy a low-cost stainless-steel sink, look for a model with the words *nickel branding*, or *302 nickel*, on the box for a minimum guaranty of longevity.

If you are shopping for an inexpensive stainless-steel kitchen sink, stay away from thin, tinny material and shallow bowls.

BUY MAJOR APPLIANCES IN THE FALL, when stores clear out old stock and are apt to offer deep discounts to make room for the latest gadget-festooned models.

Acrylic sinks are affordable and come in a wide variety of colors and configurations. But keep in mind that they are susceptible to damage from high heat, petroleum products, and abrasive cleaners. On the other hand, a light sanding with fine emery cloth and buffing with car wax can make a sink look as good as new.

FAUCETS

You may have heard that home centers carry a lower-quality, lower-priced version of the products offered through pricier plumbing showrooms. That's not true. If the product brand name and model are the same, save yourself some dough and buy it at the national chain. What chains do have is their own proprietary brands. For example, nearly identical faucets are made by Jado®, at $700, and Pegasus®, a Home Depot® brand, at $169. There are also bargains to be had in imported Chinese plumbing products, available in most large cities and on the Internet. These look like domestic and European brands, are well made, and cost about half as much.

APPLIANCES

Today, most cooks rely more on the stovetop than the oven, so it's worth considering a high-quality stove. It should have enough room for at least one large pot and come with both high-heat and ultra-low-heat burners. Choose either gas or electric, depending on your preference. Electric ranges cost less to install, but some cooks like the responsiveness of gas. Consider an induction cooktop if you have small children, because only the cookware heats up, not the burner. They also are highly energy efficient, although they cost more initially.

A freestanding range, combining cooktop and oven into one appliance, is the least expensive alternative. Even with gas burners and a convection oven, a high-end freestanding range will save you a good deal over separate units.

Unless you are an avid baker, don't rush to buy a double oven. New oven technology allows you to vary temperatures quickly so you can prepare a succession of dishes for an ambitious meal. To keep food hot as you prepare another course, install a warming drawer for about half the price of an oven. There also are microwaves that double as convection ovens for those rare occasions when you want to both broil and bake simultaneously.

Before selecting individual appliances, decide on one style for the sake of consistency. While cabinets and countertops can vary in color throughout the kitchen, I have yet to see a designer recommend that a homeowner buy a white refrigerator, a black stove, and

Iceboxes don't have to be eyesores. For a price, you can recess a refrigerator-freezer pair into a bank of cabinets.

Instead of shelling out big buck for a new fridge, consider one of the whimsical appliqué finish kits from Frigo™. You can choose chalk board, as show, stainless steel and a variety of other high end (low cost) finishes.

a stainless-steel dishwasher. My preference is for black or stainless steel because these colors remain uniform from one brand to another. That makes it easy to mix price points and manufacturers without creating a hodgepodge.

When comparing dishwashers, forget about fancy accessories such as plate warmers and delayed starts. Get a hardworking appliance with plenty of loading capacity. And if possible, pick a quiet model, because quiet and quality go together. To achieve rattle-free performance, manufacturers use better ball bearings, a sturdier frame, and thicker insulation (which improves energy efficiency as well). You may have noticed that less expensive dishwashers usually offer better energy ratings because they have fewer features and don't consume as much hot water. So look for the quietest dishwasher among the least expensive models you can find.

Certain refrigerator brands have become icons of ostentation, like Rolex® or Ferrari®. They do more for your reputation than they do for your groceries. Instead of a $5,000 status symbol, consider a model one-tenth the price and recess it into the wall for a high-end look.

Refinishing Appliances

If your appliances remain serviceable but look outdated, you may be able to renew their appearance with electrostatic painting. Some auto body shops even offer the service. Professional appliance refinishing companies will come to your house to do the work, so consult your local phone book. The finish they apply is a durable epoxy, which is factory tough and indistinguishable from new.

BUILD A BETTER BATHROOM

The second most remodeled room in the house is also usually the smallest—the

While a new kitchen usually cannot be regarded as an investment, a midrange bathroom remodeling may return about 2 percent over cost at sale, according to REMODELING Magazine**'s "Cost vs. Value Report."**

You might also choose a handheld showerhead, such as the Grohe® Movario® hand shower system shown here.

In an older home, a good alternative for spa showering is a single large rain head, such this one by Harrington® Brass Works.

bathroom. Many measure just 5 ft. by 8 ft., the minimum required to accommodate a tub, vanity, and toilet. Turning 40 sq. ft. into a room that feels more spa than latrine is a challenge, in part because you can't very well remove a wall to share space with an adjacent room. But take heart. The bathroom happens to be the most profitable room to remodel.

You can make a master bathroom a little more gracious and spacious by moving the sink into the bedroom or into an adjoining closet. A luxurious shower can occupy the same space once used by a cramped 5-ft. tub. To separate the lavatory from the toilet without chopping up the bathroom, build a low, 40-in.-high wall between them. A skylight and improved lighting will do a lot to make the room feel airy and bright. A new floor with a diagonal pattern will have a room-stretching effect. Large mirrors not only make it easier to dress but also seem to move the walls back.

A Bathroom Split

In the standard bathroom, everything is crowded together in one space, making it impossible or awkward for two people to use. A common reconfiguration isolates the toilet and tub while opening up the sink to an adjacent area.

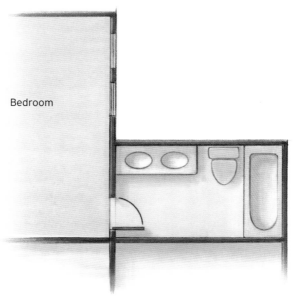

Bedroom

BEFORE

Unless you have extremely high water pressure and volume, a bank of showerheads will prove a disappointment, promising a cascade but delivering a trickle.

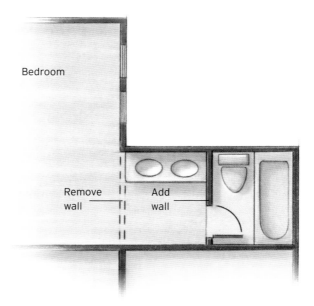

Bedroom

Remove wall

Add wall

AFTER

One way to deal with a small bathroom is to bump the shower into an adjacent closet. Studying your floor plan may suggest out-of-the-ordinary solutions such as this.

A stock pantry cabinet can serve as an ample linen closet for towels, sheets, and pillowcases in a guest room. The glass lettering was made with alphabet stencils and hobby-shop spray frosting.

Photo courtesy of Soterra

Tubs and Showers

A popular low-cost remodeling solution for a bathroom includes an acrylic tub and three-piece surround. You can buy a high-quality tub with insulation to keep the water warm and a durable finish that cleans easily. And replacement tub surrounds are generally of a higher grade than those used in new construction. Because surrounds come in pieces, you can carry them through doors and install in them in tight quarters. Some snap together, requiring no caulk to seal the seams. Just note that an acrylic surround is likely to be stronger than fiberglass, which should be installed with wood blocking for support.

A three- or four-part shower stall consists of a base and wall panels. It can be installed easily against an existing or newly framed wall. The better acrylic products keep their shape over time without deforming, while less expensive fiberglass units require backing. Several manufacturers offer tub and shower surrounds that you can place above an existing tub or shower pan.

ThinSlabZ™ is a thin stone veneer you can place directly over a firm surface, such as ceramic tile.

Lightweight Fiberock® cuts and nails like dry-wall, but there is no need to add waterproofing behind it. Just caulk the corners and set tile.

Ceramic Tile

If you like tile, the easiest and least expensive approach to a new installation involves starting with an acrylic bathtub or shower base, rather than a site-built base, and then lining the walls with a lightweight tile backer, such as Georgia-Pacific® DensShield®. This stiff gypsum board is waterproof and easy to cut, so all you do is caulk the corners and apply the tile.

Resurfacing and Repair

An old-fashioned claw tub makes bathing an especially pleasurable experience because of its deep sides and generous length. If you have a battered cast-iron tub that you'd rather not replace, consider hiring a contractor to reglaze it for a like-new finish. This involves painting the tub with an epoxy, sometimes applied to the old surface electrostatically. However, the finish typically only lasts five to 15 years or so before it begins to peel.

A more durable and more expensive solution is to install an acrylic tub liner molded to fit inside the tub with a front apron that covers the old fixture entirely. These units last a lifetime. Manufacturers offer wall panels as well. As an added bonus, the extra layer has an insulating effect so your bath water stays hot longer. Similar units are available for shower stalls.

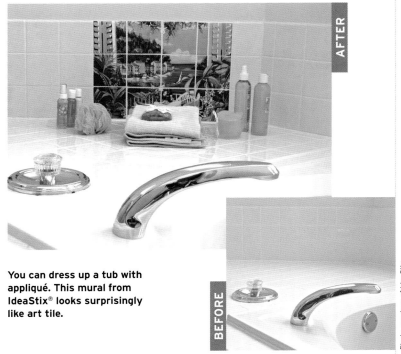

You can help compensate for uneven walls and a wavy floor by picture-framing the floor and wall with a level, square decorative pattern set in tile. It isn't noticeable in the photograph, but the floor tiles in this bathroom taper severely to accommodate out-of-square walls.

AFTER

BEFORE

AFTER

BEFORE

You can dress up a tub with appliqué. This mural from IdeaStix® looks surprisingly like art tile.

Photo courtesy of IdeaStix

You can have a sink or tub refinished with a coating that lasts anywhere from 5 years to 15 years, with the results shown in these before-and-after photos. Refinishing is especially helpful in restoring attractive old claw-foot tubs.

A brass rail, porcelain showerhead, and sheer curtain provide an affordable way to create a shower over a freestanding cast-iron tub.

Costing about a third the price of replacement, a tub or shower liner will provide the same durability as a new installation. Think of it as reupholstering the bathroom; the liner is not a paint that wears out but a new surface overlay.

If you have a beautiful shower, show it off with a transparent shower door (far right). If you have a plain acrylic surround (or simply want privacy), then shift the focus to the glass itself with an attractive glue-chip, etched, or fluted-glass enclosure (right).

Whirlpools

As a builder, I caution my clients against spending money on a whirlpool tub. Like grand pianos and exercise bicycles, they tend to sit idle. Eventually, the jets may get plugged with hard water deposits, meaning maintenance headaches. Instead, purchase a tub of adequate length and depth for your height, perhaps with armrests and a sloped back. It should cost you less than half the price of a whirlpool.

Still, if you want a jet tub, the best ones blow air instead of water, allowing you to add old-fashioned bubble bath and bathing salts and oils without damaging the jets. And you can also blow the jets clean after draining the tub, which reduces the chance of bacterial growth.

Saving Water

Showerheads are limited by law to delivering no more than 2½ gal. per minute (gpm) of water at 80 psi of pressure. But you can get around this by installing multiple heads. Although I'm sure some people find this invigorating, I found a multiple-head shower annoying.

Nevertheless, if you like being splashed from all directions, check your water pressure to make sure that multiple showerheads will work in your home. Many people have installed these only to experience a disappointing dribble from each spray head. Most bathrooms—especially in old houses—do not have enough water pressure or volume to make a modern, multihead assault shower work passably well.

Set the showerhead at 6 ft. or higher, so the water streams on your scalp not on your neck. Install a nice, high-quality, low-flow, wide-spray head with multiple settings.

Shower Doors

In a small bathroom, sliding shower doors work better than swinging doors because they take up much less space, cost less to install, and are more forgiving. Even if your measurements are a little off from standard, the overlap between panes can absorb the discrepancy without requiring a custom unit.

If you like the sleek, clean look of frameless doors, you might not like it as much

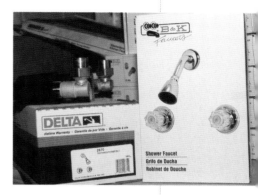

Look for bargains in quality "short-line" products carried by manufacturers that concentrate on a limited number of styles rather than offering innovation. B&K®, as an example, makes the exact faucet as Delta® for about one-third less.

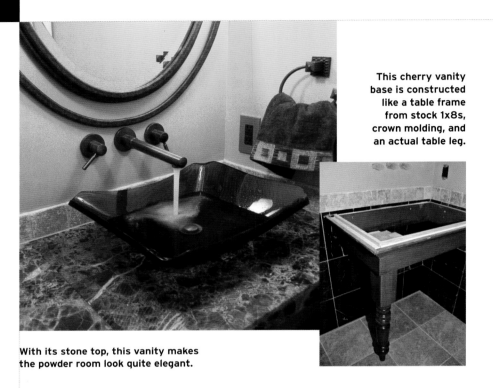

This cherry vanity base is constructed like a table frame from stock 1x8s, crown molding, and an actual table leg.

With its stone top, this vanity makes the powder room look quite elegant.

This pretty pedestal sink was made by setting a basin into a small end table. Your attic or a local antiques store might turn up a similarly charming base.

There are three general categories of bathroom lavatories: cast iron, vitreous china, and porcelain-coated pressed steel. For most applications, vitreous china represents the best choice. Coated steel is cheaper, but it chips and dents too easily.

when you discover the heavy ⅜-in. to ½-in. glass required costs three times more than standard ¼ in. glass. Instead of spending a small fortune to eliminate the frame, reduce it using a semi-frameless unit. The look is almost as clean, but not overpriced.

Vanities and Sinks

If your remodeling includes a powder room, consider installing a pedestal sink. It costs more than a standard vanity sink, but much less than a sink, vanity, and counter. This works best in a bathroom that already has adequate storage. A pedestal keeps the floor area more open, helping make a small room seem somewhat larger. To stash things, you can use a toilet-top cabinet, recessed medicine cabinet, or just wicker baskets.

Because bathroom vanity tops are smaller than kitchen counters, you can be freer to explore somewhat expensive materials. You might even be able to find a stone remnant from a marble fabricator for under $100. If your budget is stingy, look at solid-surface and cultured marble tops with integrated bowls.

A small vanity is an excellent first project if you want to try your hand at fabricating a concrete counter; see "Simple Concrete Countertop" on p. 185. An old bureau can serve as an exceptionally attractive vanity: Cut an oval in the top for a self-rimming lavatory, or set a basin sink on top after drilling a hole for the drain line.

When faucet shopping, don't restrict yourself to name brands. Store chains may carry lesser-known house brands that are good

When my clients head off to the lumberyard, cabinet shop, plumbing supply store, or lighting showroom, I warn them against selecting the best products in every category. Instead, I suggest they look for three criteria: appearance, durability, and function. Weigh each of these relative to your needs. For example, if I were shopping for a countertop, I might look for appearance first. Function and durability would come first in choosing an air-conditioning system, with little or no consideration for appearances. Durability matters most when something goes behind the wall, such as a shower valve that would be a hassle to replace.

quality, if more basic in design. For example, B&K faucets are manufactured in China from expired Delta® patents and cost about a third the price of the original.

Be aware that some manufacturers sell faucet bodies, handles, and drains separately to allow you to mix and match colors or finishes to your personal taste. This may lead you to buying an incomplete faucet thinking it's a bargain, only to have to go back to purchase the rest of the unit.

Mirrors

In a powder room or over a very traditional vanity, try an old wardrobe mirror. To make a bathroom look larger and brighter, have a glazer install a custom high-quality ¼-in. plate mirror cut to the size you need. It

If your vanity is not constrained on either of two sides, and the back wall is nice and straight, you can pick up a cheap, Chinese manufactured granite countertop in sizes ranging from 22 in. deep by 25 in., 31 in., 37 in., or 49 in. long The top comes cut for a standard 19 in. oval sink and 4 in. spread faucet. Ranging in price from $89 to $259, these tops can be found at major home improvement centers.

Photo courtesy of Mirr.Edge

Clear acrylic or wood-grain mirror-edge finishes by Mirr.Edge offer an easy fix for a mirror that has begun to show its age around the edges.

Don't scrimp on a bathroom fan. A high-quality, whisper-quiet model like this Panasonic® will help keep a bathroom dry and well ventilated.

will have more impact than an inexpensive precut mirror.

If you have a mirror that is serviceable but shabby, consider reframing it with hardwood or a paintable door casing. Or use Mirr.Edge™, an edging product that makes it simple to construct a new frame. Just score the framing material with a utility knife and snap it to length.

A common reason for undertaking a bathroom remodeling is the damage caused by moisture—mold, mildew, and crumbling drywall. Don't skimp when shopping for an exhaust fan. A good-quality fan will do a better job of venting moisture to the outdoors and will perform more quietly.

Extractors and Humidity

One of the reasons you might be remodeling your bath is the presence of mold,

mildew, and rotten drywall—the destructive forces of nature that assemble in every bathroom. They are the reasons why you should never skimp on a good-quality exhaust fan. A quality fan removes all the moisture in your bathroom within about three minutes. The best fans work so quietly that you need an indicator light to know if they are running. They do cost more, however. Although I like quiet, I'd rather save a few dollars and step down to a fan like the Panasonic® Whisper Ceiling Mounted Fan, which runs at ½ sones, half as quiet as your refrigerator. A good fan will exhaust unpleasant odors quickly, remove humid air when you bathe, and it will do it all without disturbing the peace. A strong word of caution here: Always exhaust your fan to the exterior, never into the attic.

The most intimate seat in the house need not be fancy, just sturdy and efficient. This simple yet stylish American Standard® model delivers on both counts.

Before beauty, look for the basics. This Eljer® bowl has internal glazing and good-quality gaskets.

THE THRONE

My advice here is short and sweet: Stay away from cheap toilets. The trapways and rim holes may not be glazed, which makes them vulnerable to clogging with waterborne minerals. Within months you may notice the diminished flushing power. Economical, well-built, two-piece fixtures with an elongated bowl, such as Kohler's Wellworth or the American Standard® Cadet II, offer a sleek profile and good flushing operation.

If you have a pre-existing problem with old pipes or slow drainage, consider a power-assist toilet. It uses compressed air to force waste down the trap. At about $100 more than a standard toilet (and they sometimes require an electric outlet), these toilets exert force on the water in the tank so that you'll be less likely to need a plunger close at hand.

Scaling Back, Not Moving Down

When Sheri and Robert Hampton became tired of taking care of a large suburban home, they moved to a smaller place in the city. Their 1960's classical revival was in a great neighborhood but the house was dated by powder blue carpeting and white melamine cabinets, 8-ft. ceilings and a cramped floor plan.

The first remodeling bids came in way over budget. So Robert hired subcontractors directly. He discovered that he could buy custom-made unfinished cherry cabinets and have them installed for about half a contractor's quote. He found that granite countertops in 18-in. by 24-in. sections would look as good as full-size slabs and cost 30 percent less. Sheri shopped for discounted floor tile, and was able to reuse carpeting from their old house because the buyer didn't like it.

Instead of paring down the remodeling by reducing the scope of work, they pared down costs through comparison shopping. It wasn't entirely a matter of nickel and diming. Robert considered putting the nearly $15,000 saved on kitchen cabinets into a retirement account, but then splurged on a professional pizza oven instead.

8 High-Impact, Low-Budget Exteriors

THE APPEARANCE OF YOUR HOME depends as much on the color and variety of materials chosen for your roofing, trim, and siding as it does on the overall architectural elements of the facade. These personal choices define what real estate agents call "curb appeal." You can build a successful, aesthetically pleasing exterior without elaborate trim or expensive finishes. Inexpensive materials—such as plywood, stucco, faux brick, fiber-cement siding, and even creatively applied vinyl siding—can achieve high-end curb-appeal. In this chapter, I show you how.

MAKING YOUR PLANS

If a simple coat of paint isn't enough to make the difference you want to see in the facade of your house, then take a digital photo of the front and print several large copies on plain bond paper. Using colored pencils and magazine clippings from siding advertisements, play around with the look of your home by gluing and coloring a variety of finishes onto the photos.

Choosing the Parts and Pieces

At first, choose accents and strategic upgrades to improve the facade without re-covering the entire structure. Often, just new siding on a gable end or an elegant band of wainscoting along the beltline will suffice to dress up the exterior. In other cases, it's necessary to re-cover the entire structure. By drawing and coloring the photos, you can easily experiment with all kinds of cladding before committing to a specific remodeling scheme.

Never select the siding for your house by choosing a single product line, such as aluminum siding or stucco. Instead, achieve a high-end look on a budget by combining several cladding materials in an eye-catching manner. Chose exterior elements compatible with the architectural style of your house; this is where an architect or talented designer can help. Although I have built and remodeled thousands of houses over a 30-year career, I still rely on the good advice of architects and talented designers when choosing an exterior scheme that both

Olive green-painted plywood and corrugated metal cladding reflect the natural hues of the Oregon landscape making a beautifully balanced exterior for the frugal remodeler.

Installed like standard lap siding, Novabrik provides a less-expensive alternative to real brick veneer and, though applied in overlapping courses like clapboard siding, presents a realistic look.

OLD LOOK, NEW PERFORMANCE

Siding used to be made of individual boards, typically 8 ft. to 12 ft. long, with each piece of siding lapped over the piece below it to provide a waterproof covering for the house. Nowadays, sheets of vinyl, hardboard, or cement board are designed to look and perform just like the old-style horizontal siding. Today's siding is available in a variety of looks from the classic, 4-in. colonial siding to 5-in. Dutch lap with a slightly rounded edge to the more modern 8-in. to 10-in. widths.

reflects and updates the best architectural characteristics of a house.

For example, the house shown on p. 215 combines a tasteful color scheme with vinyl siding and an inexpensive concrete brick often used on commercial buildings. What allows these materials to work well in a high-end application is the careful choice of color and variety; by detailing the vinyl siding with wider-than-normal trim, and blending three different brick colors to achieve a natural, variegated appearance, the designers created a satisfying exterior

VINYL SIDING

Because this book is about saving money, let's start with the most economical means of cladding your house besides a good coat of paint. Vinyl siding is often maligned by architects and green building advocates because it can look. . .well. . .cheap; and the manufacture of polyvinyl chloride (PVC), has deleterious effects on the environment. However, vinyl siding has sufficient environmental offsets that it is permitted even by the most stringent green building standards, such as The Leadership in Energy and Environmental Design (LEED[SM]) Green Building Rating System, a nationally accepted benchmark for the design, construction, and operation of high-performance green buildings. In short, vinyl siding never needs paint; it's easy to maintain; and once installed, there's no added expense.

Use Details to Make It Yours

On the aesthetic front, vinyl siding is now available in a wide selection of trim, period colors, and other traditional building elements created to match specific historic styles. When you choose a higher-grade material with a fade-resistant finish and a full complement of traditional laps and trim, you can achieve the award-winning looks found in many architecturally notable, neo-Traditional neighborhoods around the country.

To create a distinguished look with vinyl, combine colors and a variety of cladding types, including the traditional narrow panels mixed with modern wider panels. I like to use deeper colors and wider panels around the first floor of the house to give it weight, then switch to narrower strips and lighter colors on the second story. I use bands of cement board to create the look of freeze board, breaking up the monotony of a blank facade.

Change the lap to distinguish architectural features such as gable ends, chimneys, and distinct masses or shapes of your house (such as a bump-out, bay, or gable). Take advantage of a contrasting color at the corners. Match the color of the J-molding around windows to the window frame color to create the illusion of thicker casing. Don't be afraid to combine different siding types, such as the painted cement-board siding shown in the photos on p. 207.

Mixing and Matching

It's common to see a house with a brick front and vinyl siding on the other three elevations, but you can also combine vinyl with cement siding or even plywood. Try to place wood finishes, such as T-11 and hardboard siding on the second story, far from sprinklers and landscape, so you can take advantage of these low-cost alternatives where they weather least. Use site-built wood, not plastic shutters, to save money and provide a more genuine finish. Don't hesitate to combine vinyl siding with wood or paintable fiberglass corners and window trim for an even more traditional appearance.

CEMENT BOARD, PLYWOOD, AND HARDBOARD

With a few exceptions, houses in this country were built with wood. And we still use a lot of wood, though nowadays we've allowed science and engineering to improve on the original and even add a few new materials. Many of these new products fall

THE BASICS OF HANGING VINYL SIDING

Installing vinyl siding on your house isn't rocket science, but following a few simple steps can ensure that the job you do looks great and performs well.

HANG LOOSE Don't nail vinyl siding tight to the wall, keep the heads of nails out about $\frac{1}{16}$ in. from the surface, otherwise the material will buckle and break as it expands and contracts.

ROOM TO MOVE Give panels room to expand and contract at the ends by leaving about a $\frac{3}{8}$-inch gap at J-channel and other abutting moldings.

HIDE YOUR BUTTS Alternate panel joints by starting construction at the opposite end from the most prominent viewing position to hide the butt end of the siding.

KEEP IT HORIZONTAL Snapping a level line every few courses will keep your siding straight and neat when viewed from the street.

WINDOW WISE Try to align full-panel widths above your most visible windows; slivers of siding above lintels look shabby. Measure down from the tops of your prominent windows to the starter strip and then make sure your courses coincide so the shadow lines of your siding line up atop the most prominent windows.

WIDER IS BETTER When it comes to corners and trim, nothing says vinyl siding louder than a narrow strip of J-channel. Instead of 1-in. J-channel, use wider window and door casing, available at a slight upgrade in price; the results will far outweigh the small added expense.

VINYL LEAKS Vinyl siding is designed to leak. The real waterproofing occurs in a "drainage plane" behind the siding. Make sure you have a continuous weather-resistant barrier and carefully crafted flashing behind your vinyl.

Some vinyl siding comes with added insulation. While not terribly significant as an insulating layer, the backing of high density foam stiffens the siding for added strength.

New vinyl products, such as the shingle style panels used on this house, provide the appearance of expensive cedar shake at vinyl prices.

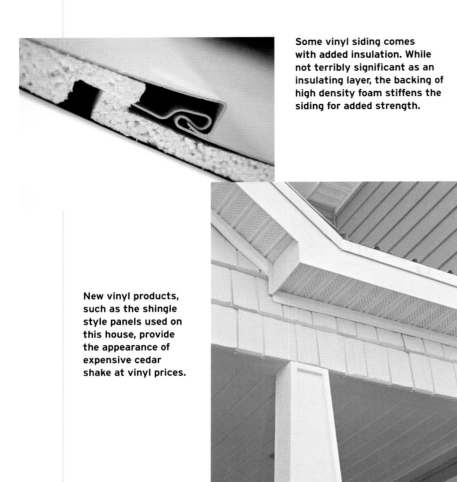

THE CASE FOR VINYL SIDING

ENERGY EFFICIENCY Vinyl siding is significantly lighter than some alternative materials, such as brick and fiber cement, which saves energy and fuel in transportation.

RECYCLING Nearly all scrap generated during the manufacturing of vinyl siding is recycled back into a finished product.

INDOOR/OUTDOOR AIR QUALITY Vinyl's ease of maintenance means no paints, stains, or harsh chemical cleaners are required.

RESOURCE CONSERVATION Vinyl siding can replace wood-based products such as cedar siding. The siding and its accessories are also durable products, which is increasingly being recognized as an advantage not only from an economic perspective but also from an environmental one. The longer a product lasts, the less energy and other resources required to maintain the product or manufacture replacements. Furthermore, less scrap ends up in the landfill.

under the heading of "engineered wood," and plywood is one early example. But newer products combine other materials with wood to produce wholly new types of building products. Cement board, for instance, is a mix of wood fibers with portland cement held together with chemical binders to create faux wood siding that should last at least 50 years. And hardboard is made from wood chips harvested from short-rotation or immature trees. The ingredients are bound with chemicals for a stable, long-lasting product that contains less phenol formaldehyde binder than plywood or OSB.

This distinctive remodel includes wide lap siding on the base, corrugated metal on the second story and a narrower lap siding on the gable end.

Cement-Based Siding

Cement-based siding boards come as clapboard planks or sheets and resemble plywood. I highly recommended them because they never rot, offer a fire-resistant alternative to masonry, and hold paint like a magnet. However, they have one drawback: Unlike vinyl, you have to paint this siding. You can find a limited range of prefinished lap siding, but the product is almost twice the price, and the installation is very exacting.

Nevertheless, I often use cement siding products to add detail like window trim,

Fiber-cement siding is made from portland cement, sand, and cellulose fiber. It comes in several styles: with a bead cut into one edge, flat and smooth or in a wood grain texture. Manufacturers guarantee their products against rot for 50 years. Nevertheless, I have never heard of cement rotting even after 5,000 years, so the siding should last you a while. If you need a solid, noncombustible cladding, or live in an area with termites, fiber-cement siding (which does not burn and resists insect, salt, and hail damage) provides a number of benefits that make it attractive in the long run.

This Michigan bungalow clad creatively with exterior plywood and 1-in. vertical battens looks a lot more interesting and "designed" than neighboring houses decked in more sober siding.

PRO TIP

IF YOU USE A WOOD PRODUCT LIKE PLYWOOD, instead of painting it, stain the siding with a high-quality, deep-penetrating solid body stain. The solid body stain will give the color depth and protection of paint, but when it comes time to recoat the house in about 5 years, you won't have to worry about scraping off peeling paint.

corners, and even discreet areas of painted siding that add dazzling color and contrast. Palettes available in prefinished materials like hardboard, vinyl, and cement have improved, but nothing compares to the variety and vitality available at the paint store. By introducing a few areas of custom color on trim and architectural elements, you can strike a balance between high style and low maintenance. I always place painted surfaces well above areas subject to sprinkler overspray, ground moisture, and salt.

Hardboard Siding That Does Not Need Paint

If you strongly dislike the use of vinyl but want a maintenance free, prefinished product, don't be afraid of the new color-integrated hardboard siding. Although hardboard had a bad reputation in the wake of highly publicized failures in the early 1990s, these early problems have been solved. New hardboard siding is made with excellent adhesive binders and weathering components that prevent it from absorbing

The gaps between these sections of fiber-cement clapboards is filled with caulk and painted over. Once the paint dries, the joint visually disappears.

Fiber-cement siding goes up on your house just like traditional beveled cedar clapboards. However, these clapboards will last indefinitely compared to their old-style wood counterparts.

The seams created by the remodel of this San Diego home disappear under a uniform topcoat of stucco. Exterior architectural details include the French doors, faux balcony, and second-floor veranda. Stucco remains one the best materials for siding because it's durable, beautiful, and virtually maintenance free. In the West and Southwest, it's also among the least expensive exterior finishes available.

Finger-jointed, factory-primed exterior trim comes with 10-year paint adhesion warranty, promising better results than you could achieve even with the most thorough prep work.

water; swelling; and, in some of those early cases, actually supporting the growth of small mushrooms. Georgia-Pacific's high-resin, all-wood fiber composite comes with warranties ranging from 10 years to 30 years, something cedar siding does not offer.

Maybe Give Real Wood a Shot

You can also buy finger-jointed pine or cedar trim boards, factory primed and carrying warranties of 10 years to 30 years (if you are also concerned about the environment, these are a good bet because they're made by invisibly joining many small off-cuts—the byproducts of siding manufacturing). But some of these products are as, or more, expensive than real wood. If you don't like artificial products and cannot afford wood, I suggest using plain, unfinished, but factory-primed hardboard siding on soffits, fascia, and upper-level areas on the house and cover them with the highest quality paints available. Compared with repainting, even the most expensive gallon of paint comes cheap.

Plywood: The First Engineered Wood Product

If you don't mind painting the surface of your home, consider exterior-grade plywood. You can buy sheets that come scored to resemble vertical plank siding, bead board, or just plain smooth wood. The joints between sheets have a shiplap overlay that makes the seams almost invisible. Many people like to install 1-in. by 2-in. vertical battens every 24 in. to better disguise and protect the seams (this touch approximates the look of traditional board-and-batten siding but comes a lot cheaper).

The good thing about plywood siding is that it provides an excellent substrate for a more elegant cladding in the future. We used plywood to side our first house with the idea that one day we would be able to afford lap siding. In fact, the house looked so good when we finished that, three owners later, it still stands as we built it; but if some future

owner wanted, the upgrade would be as simple as if the house were still under construction—simply apply the new siding on top of the old.

DON'T SNEER AT STUCCO

In some parts of the country—the West Coast for instance—stucco siding is still made with real cement. In most of the rest of the country, however, the heavy and labor-intensive material has been supplanted by synthetic stucco, generally called exterior insulation and finish systems (EIFS). While applying real stucco usually is the province of experienced tradespeople, equally rigorous application standards apply to synthetic stucco.

The "Real" Stucco

So-called three-coat stucco is an excellent cladding. If you live in an area like southern California, where plasterers are plentiful, it's also relatively cheap. In other parts of the country, only the richest of the rich can afford it. Which is too bad, because stucco not only affords a maintenance-free exterior but adds structural value and provides exceptional fire protection. Still, when used in large spans without variation it becomes as tedious as any other siding, which is why I like to mix up the materials on my exteriors. Stucco was seemingly made to create distinctive exterior features because it can easily be molded, carved, and colored.

If you live in a stucco house and want to add brick accents, such as a brick chimney, you can achieve the look easily through one of my favorite faux brick techniques. Power-wash the existing stucco surface and trowel on a ⅜-in.-thick adhesive coat of gray mortar. If adhesion is a problem, first coat the wall with a ⅛-in. layer of waterproof thin set, the type used for tile installation. Once the gray (or brown coat, as it's called in the trades) dries, follow up with a ¼-in.-thick color coat of red stucco finish. Before the color coat has a chance to set, carve lines into the top layer with a ½-in. tuck-pointing

Red top-coat stucco carved with a tuck-pointing trowel provides a convincing, brick-like finish on this otherwise boring, stucco chimney.

When properly installed, synthetic stucco can remain trouble free for decades. However, this photo shows the problem that can result from defective workmanship. From the outside, the house looked great, but after water got inside the house envelope, the story inside the walls wasn't so pretty.

THREE-LAYER SYNTHETIC STUCCO

FIRST LAYER Insulation board, made of polystyrene or polyisocyanurate foam and covered with a fiberglass mesh, is secured to the exterior wall surface and with a specially formulated adhesive and/or mechanical fastener.

SECOND LAYER A water-resistant base coat is applied on top of the insulation and fiberglass mesh for added strength.

THIRD LAYER A top coat, typically a cement-acrylic copolymer layer, is troweled on for a colorfast and crack-resistant finish.

Alternating between the rough texture created by using a sponge trowel and the slick finish achieved by a steel trowel can render details like these *quoins,* **which look like the traditional stacked interlocking blocks at the corners of a masonry building.**

trowel (available at any home improvement store), revealing the gray mortar lines underneath. The finish is almost indistinguishable from brick. You can also carve this color coat with a striking tool to outline window frames and render architectural features such as keystones and embossed corners.

Modern-Day Stucco

The modern stucco alternative was developed in Europe in the 1950s as a quick and easy means of repairing plaster facades ravaged during World War II. The product was introduced to North America in the 1980s as EIFS. A multilayered exterior wall sandwich, EIFS goes more quickly than three-coat stucco and without much of a mess. It's composed of three layers: The first layer consists of high-density insulation board nailed over the framing (instead of lath and two coats of plaster), followed by a fiberglass mesh that's nailed to the insulation board. The mesh acts as the metal or wood lath in the old-style stucco and is covered in a quick-drying topcoat of portland cement and latex, which has the color mixed throughout.

Over the last 30 years, the product has been applied to both commercial buildings and homes and now accounts for about 30 percent of the stucco market. But it was not originally successful. Because of the latex and foam, EFIS forms a watertight siding system that does not breathe. That might seem ideal—after all it keeps out the water, which is what you want. However, the old system suffered from an Achilles' heel: Water that managed to get in (usually through poorly caulked windows), couldn't get out. After a while, rot and mold occurred.

Newer EIFS is just as waterproof but now includes a drainage arrangement behind the siding so that if water gets behind the synthetic stucco the system allows it to drain harmlessly out. If you're interested in this system for your remodel, ask a trusted home builder for details about contemporary EIFS.

When applied properly, the system looks great and provides the added benefit of an extra layer of insulation. It can be vulnerable to impacts, such as hail, an errant baseball, or woodpecker damage. The long-term performance or short-term failure of this system depends on the quality of the installation.

EIFS is not a do-it-yourself wall cladding. It should be installed only by experienced applicators who have completed an EIFS manufacturer's training program; thus the system can be more expensive than traditional stucco. You can find qualified installers through the EIFS manufacture of your choice or on the EIFS Industry Members Association (EIMA) Web site (www.eima.com).

MASONRY MAGIC

Unlike vinyl siding, plywood, and even stucco, precast concrete stone products have become respectable elements in architecturally high-end exteriors. People who otherwise would never dream of applying any artificial material to their house stick on portland cement imitation ledger rock without hesitation. Manufacturers have developed colors unavailable in nature to suit decorator tastes.

I don't know why, but stick-on stone has become perhaps the most popular artificial siding product ever invented. Perhaps because, since antiquity, the hardness and durability of stone represented the best in building materials. A good stone house, each block cut smooth and well fitted, looks as if it could last for centuries. And although the stonemason's art has largely disappeared from the modern-day world of production housing, our love for the random mosaic of nature's first building material endures. It's the quaint stone cottages and the grand stone castles of Europe that we covet. It's the brawny texture and the subtle, variegated colors of stonework that we long to call home.

But natural stone has become prohibitive for a number of reasons, including the lack of good stonemasons and the expense of quarrying and transporting it. So, it's not

Even an up-close look will fool the eye when it comes to this lightweight concrete cast and colored manufactured-stone veneer, which costs a fraction of real stone.

Metal lath is screwed to plywood and then covered with a thin layer of mortar in preparation for attaching lightweight concrete stone veneer to the foundation of this house.

surprising that builders and homeowners have turned to artificial stone products to satisfy their aesthetic and budget requirements. The good news is that best manufactured stone no longer looks artificial. Molded from bona-fide quarried stone and fieldstone, some manufactured products have become virtually indistinguishable from the real thing. Manufacturers can ship these light, and easily packaged stones long distances, and they provide scores of rock types, textures, colors, and styles

for just about anywhere in the United States. But despite the ready availability of a variety of looks, for the most genuine appearance, try finding stones that look as if they were found within 100 miles of your home.

Most of this book details *what to do* as opposed to *how to do it*, but because setting artificial stone is so simple and painless, I include a short section on how to apply it. You can install manufactured stone over most construction surfaces—indoors or

WHEN USING CULTURED STONE CARRY THE STONE COURSE AROUND THE CORNER for a realistic appearance. Wash the stone with grout to obtain a gritty, older look, and add chips of terra-cotta tile to the grout for texture.

out. You don't need wall-ties, footings, or special structural support even in earth-quake zones. There's no substrate prepara-tion required to install manufactured stone over clean and untreated concrete or ma-sonry surfaces. But on building surfaces such as wood studs, plywood, and drywall, you have to construct a rigid mud-base substrate similar to that needed for installing split brick or ceramic tile.

Paving the Way

To prepare the surface over open studs, you'll need to apply paper-backed galva-nized ¾-in. expanded metal lath fastened to the studs using galvanized nails or staples. Nail the lath every 6 in. vertically along the studs using nails that provide at least 1 in. penetration. Lath comes in sheets about 27 in. wide by 96 in. long. Overlap the paper about 2 in. horizontally and vertically, and the metal lath by at least 1 in. This is easy to do, because the paper and lath come shiplapped so that you can lay one course over the other, and end to end, paper lapping paper and metal without the need to cut or modify the sheets. Then apply a ½-in.-thick scratch coat of mortar over the lath and allow it to cure 48 hours before installing the stone.

Over wallboard, plywood, or rigid insula-tion board, start by covering the wall with a weather-resistant barrier, such as waterproof kraft building paper or asphalt-saturated rag felt. Apply the weather barrier horizontally, overlapping the succeeding upward layers by at least 2 in. and by 6 in. at the ends. Install 2½-lb. or heavier diamond-mesh

expanded, galvanized metal lath over this barrier using galvanized nails or staples 6 in. on-center vertically and 16 in. hori-zontally. Make sure the nails penetrate the framing by at least 1 in. Overlap the mesh at least ½ in. on the sides and 1 in. at the ends. Double-wrap the metal lath at all the inside and outside corners. Apply a ½-in. scratch coat of mortar over the lath and allow it to set.

Laying It Up

Before you start mortaring stones onto the wall, lay out about 25 sq. ft. of the stone on the ground near your work area. This allows you to play with the fit and color pattern before you set the stones in place. You'll want a balanced pattern of shapes, sizes, and colors on the wall. It's easier to do this when you have a pallet to choose from, instead of just grabbing whatever stone comes next from the box.

Unlike other masonry, you should install most manufactured stone from the top down. The material is light enough to stick without support, and by starting at the top you avoid dripping mortar onto your work. On a dry-stack installation, you'll still have to install courses from the bottom up, work-ing carefully to avoid staining the stone with the mortar.

Whichever way you go, install your corner pieces before you get started on the wall surface. This makes it easier to fit the rest of the stones, or "flats," into place later. Corner pieces come in short and long L-shaped lengths. By alternating these on the corner, you achieve a look more like the real thing, which is fairly irregular. Although stones do vary in size, you can still use a level or a plumb line to make sure the corners are true.

When working with quarried stone styles, you'll need to keep the courses level. Snap chalk lines every 4 in. to 8 in. as an eyeball guide, and then use a torpedo level to set each piece.

Getting Natural-Looking Joints

Don't forget to stagger the joints both vertically and horizontally. Stones look best with uniform grout lines of about ½ in. or less. Avoid long, unbroken grout lines when placing fieldstone, river rock, and other variably sized stones.

You can cut and shape stones with a brick hatchet, wide-mouth nippers or your trowel edge. For long, straight cuts use a circular saw with a diamond masonry blade. Al-

though good-quality manufactured stone has color all the way through, you should always turn any cut edges away from sight lines. In other words, when you install a cut stone below eye level, turn the cut-side down. Above eye level, turn it up.

To apply mortar using a mason's trowel, butter the back of each stone with a ½ -in.-thick layer of mortar and, using a gentle wiggling action, press the stone firmly into place. It's okay to allow a little mortar to squeeze out along the sides of the stone. After your stone has set, carefully apply mortar between the stones using a grout bag (home centers or masonry supply stores carry these; using one is like making French pastry), taking care not to smear grout onto the stone surface. Once the mortar joints have become firm (about 30 minutes to 60 minutes), use a wooden or metal striking tool to rake out the

Certain faux siding combinations just don't look natural. When trying to fake it with faux masonry, beams, and stone, try to use products that actually resemble traditional construction combinations. For instance, a stone foundation with lap siding above it would look more natural than a stone foundation with modular brick siding.

excess mortar. Work grout into the joints, and thoroughly seal the edges.

After working the grout lines, use a whisk broom to smooth the joints and clean off loose mortar. At this point, brush off any drops and spots, which should come up easily. Never use a damp sponge to clean the surface, or you'll stain the stone permanently. Do not use a wire brush, acid, or harsh cleaner. It's not necessary to seal manufactured stone, since it weathers like natural rock. But some people like to deepen the colors with a high-quality, penetrating masonry sealer. Sealers help keep the stone clean where exposed to mud or soot. But always test the sealer on a sample piece because it will change the stone's appearance.

FAUX DOESN'T MEAN FUNKY

Unlike artificial stone, which has become an accepted and even desirable cladding, artificial brick lags in popular acceptance—perhaps because the old rolls of asphalt shingle-style bricks and the squares of cork-like brick composite looked so fake, whereas modern concrete stone looks real. You might want to revisit some of the "real" brick surfaces in your neighborhood, because a few of them might just be the new and improved faux brick, like the Nichiha™ products used in historical rehabilitation. Flexi-Brick™ facing, which cuts with scissors and installs easily over almost any smooth, sound surface, is also available. The finished product is virtually indistinguishable from the real thing.

For a true brick facing at a lower cost, you can purchase thin brick, or split brick, which is nothing more than tile-deep slivers of real clay brick that you place against a sound substrate, just as you would artificial stone. Some thin brick comes on a mesh backing, like mosaic tile, so you can install large areas without fussing over the grout lines. Thin brick requires more skill to install than artificial veneers, however,

Novabrik installed on this house in my hometown cost about $4 per square foot, including materials and labor. Although the installation looks professional, the men working here had never used the product before.

especially when it comes to grouting. But with care and patience, you can achieve professional results.

Mortarless Brick

For the bold, solid feeling of genuine masonry without the technical difficulty, try one of the mortarless brick alternatives, such as Novabrik, which you or a siding crew can install quickly and easily right over existing siding at a fraction of the cost of ordinary brickwork. The men installing Novabrik on the front of the house in the photo above are not masons or siding installers by trade, but painters.

Index